How Does Video Game Violence Affect Society?

Other titles in the *In Controversy* series:

Are Video Games Harmful?

Can Renewable Energy Replace Fossil Fuels?

Childhood Obesity

Does the Death Penalty Deter Crime?

Does Illegal Immigration Harm Society?

How Dangerous Are Performance-Enhancing Drugs?

How Does Cell Phone Use Impact Teenagers?

How Serious a Problem Is Drug Use in Sports?

How Serious a Threat Is Climate Change?

How Should America Respond to Illegal Immigration?

How Should Sex Education Be Taught in Schools?

How Should the World Respond to Global Warming?

Identity Theft

Is Animal Experimentation Ethical?

Is Human Embryo Experimentation Ethical?

Is Medical Marijuana Necessary?

Is Offshore Oil Drilling Worth the Risks?

Is Social Networking Beneficial to Society?

Is Stem Cell Research Necessary?

Is the World Prepared for a Deadly Influenza Pandemic?

Should the Drinking Age Be Lowered?

Should Juveniles Be Tried as Adults?

Should Marijuana Be Legalized?

Should Smoking Be Banned?

How Does Video Game Violence Affect Society?

Patricia D. Netzley

INCONTROVERSY

ReferencePoint
Press®

© 2013 ReferencePoint Press, Inc.
Printed in the United States

For more information, contact:
ReferencePoint Press, Inc.
PO Box 27779
San Diego, CA 92198
www.ReferencePointPress.com

LIBRARY OF CONGRESS CATALOGING-IN-PUBLICATION DATA

Netzley, Patricia D.
 How does video game violence affect society? / by Patricia D. Netzley.
  p. cm. -- (In controversy series)
 Includes bibliographical references and index.
 ISBN 978-1-60152-490-4 (hbk.) -- ISBN 1-60152-490-0 (hbk.) 1. Violence in video games--Juvenile literature. 2. Video games--Social aspects--Juvenile literature. 3. Video games--Psychological aspects--Juvenile literature. 4. Violence--Juvenile literature. I. Title.
 GV1469.34.V56N48   2013
 794.8--dc23
                                                2012031924

Contents

Foreword

In 2008, as the US economy and economies worldwide were falling into the worst recession since the Great Depression, most Americans had difficulty comprehending the complexity, magnitude, and scope of what was happening. As is often the case with a complex, controversial issue such as this historic global economic recession, looking at the problem as a whole can be overwhelming and often does not lead to understanding. One way to better comprehend such a large issue or event is to break it into smaller parts. The intricacies of global economic recession may be difficult to understand, but one can gain insight by instead beginning with an individual contributing factor, such as the real estate market. When examined through a narrower lens, complex issues become clearer and easier to evaluate.

This is the idea behind ReferencePoint Press's *In Controversy* series. The series examines the complex, controversial issues of the day by breaking them into smaller pieces. Rather than looking at the stem cell research debate as a whole, a title would examine an important aspect of the debate such as *Is Stem Cell Research Necessary?* or *Is Embryonic Stem Cell Research Ethical?* By studying the central issues of the debate individually, researchers gain a more solid and focused understanding of the topic as a whole.

Each book in the series provides a clear, insightful discussion of the issues, integrating facts and a variety of contrasting opinions for a solid, balanced perspective. Personal accounts and direct quotes from academic and professional experts, advocacy groups, politicians, and others enhance the narrative. Sidebars add depth to the discussion by expanding on important ideas and events. For quick reference, a list of key facts concludes every chapter. Source notes, an annotated organizations list, bibliography, and index provide student researchers with additional tools for papers and class discussion.

The *In Controversy* series also challenges students to think critically about issues, to improve their problem-solving skills, and to sharpen their ability to form educated opinions. As President Barack Obama stated in a March 2009 speech, success in the twenty-first century will not be measurable merely by students' ability to "fill in a bubble on a test but whether they possess 21st century skills like problem-solving and critical thinking and entrepreneurship and creativity." Those who possess these skills will have a strong foundation for whatever lies ahead.

No one can know for certain what sort of world awaits today's students. What we can assume, however, is that those who are inquisitive about a wide range of issues; open-minded to divergent views; aware of bias and opinion; and able to reason, reflect, and reconsider will be best prepared for the future. As the international development organization Oxfam notes, "Today's young people will grow up to be the citizens of the future: but what that future holds for them is uncertain. We can be quite confident, however, that they will be faced with decisions about a wide range of issues on which people have differing, contradictory views. If they are to develop as global citizens all young people should have the opportunity to engage with these controversial issues."

In Controversy helps today's students better prepare for tomorrow. An understanding of the complex issues that drive our world and the ability to think critically about them are essential components of contributing, competing, and succeeding in the twenty-first century.

An Obsession with Violence

On April 9, 2011, twenty-four-year-old Tristan van der Vlis went to a busy mall in the town of Alphen aan den Rijn, Netherlands, with a semiautomatic rifle, a .45 caliber pistol, and a .44 Magnum revolver. He then fired over a hundred bullets into the crowd, killing six people and wounding seventeen before killing himself. His victims included children and senior citizens.

In trying to determine the reason for the shooting, experts have pointed to many different aspects of the killer's life. Van der Vlis had a history of psychiatric problems and had tried to commit suicide at least twice prior to his death. A member of a shooting club, he was also enamored of guns and managed to purchase the semiautomatic rifle despite the fact that the possession of such weapons is illegal in Netherlands. But what has attracted the most attention is Van der Vlis's obsession with a violent video game.

Specifically, friends of the killer came forward after the massacre to say that Van der Vlis had spent hours playing the game *Call of Duty: Modern Warfare 2*, and police confirmed this by studying his computer. Once this fact became known, media reports began to note that one component of the game, a mission commonly known as the Airport Massacre, has features that are similar to Van der Vlis's mall massacre. The goal of this mission is for the player, in the role of an uncover agent working with terrorists, to gun down as many innocent civilians as possible in an airport terminal, and Van der Vlis's movements during the massacre were similar to those a player would make as the shooter within the game environment. In addition, at the end of the level the shooter dies, although he is killed by the terrorists rather than himself.

Calls for Bans

When such connections arise, calls for the banning of violent video games increase. But experts disagree not only on whether such bans should be enacted but also on whether violent video games deserve banning. Some say the games are harmless; others insist they condition and train people to kill. There are also those who say that even if violent video games do teach players skills that will enable them to accurately aim and shoot a real gun, such games still do not deserve blame in cases like Van der Vlis's. For example, Paul Tassi, who writes about video games, technology, and the Internet for *Forbes* magazine, says that even if such a shooter "went to a gun range every single day for the past year, a place that actually trains you how to hit person-shaped targets with a real gun firing real bullets in your hands, would we be talking about how shooting ranges are to blame? Would we want them all closed down for fear someone else might learn how to shoot a gun and kill someone?"[1]

Ratings and Warnings

Nonetheless, lawmakers have attempted to limit young people's access to violent games, and the video game industry has adopted a ratings system for games that warns parents when the content is inappropriate for children. Some warnings also appear within games, alerting players that violent content is coming. For example, the popular *Call of Duty: Modern Warfare 2* warns players that certain missions could be disturbing and provides them with the choice of skipping the mission without being penalized in terms of achievements or game completion. In order to proceed through the game, players must click "yes" or "no" to indicate whether they want to skip these missions.

But despite such precautions, some experts say that violent games should not even be sold, given that adults like Van der Vlis can be influenced by them. Indeed, recent evidence indicates that males in their teens and twenties are the most affected by game violence. For example, in 2011 a study by the Indiana University School of Medicine suggested that playing violent video games can make men aged eighteen to twenty-nine less able to control their anger.

Antisocial Behavior

Yet young men seem particularly drawn to violent video games. According to recent surveys, the most popular video game among young males is *Grand Theft Auto*, which allows players to act out many types of criminal behavior—including brutally murdering police officers—and is widely considered one of the most violent games on the market. (In contrast, among young females the most popular game is *The Sims*, which features a virtual house and its inhabitants going about their daily lives.) There are several versions of *Grand Theft Auto*, and all of them have been criticized for glorifying criminal acts. In fact, in 2009 the Gamer's Edition of *The Guinness Book of World Records* decreed *Grand Theft Auto* the world's most controversial video game.

Such games typically allow players to act out bad behavior, and some experts say this encourages the same kind of antisocial be-

Two girls embrace beside flowers and a sign that asks, "Why?" outside a Netherlands shopping mall where Tristan van der Vlis killed six people and wounded seventeen. The media reported similarities between the shooting and a mission featured in a video game that van der Vlis often played.

havior in the offline world. One of the most outspoken proponents of the notion that online violence leads to offline violence is Jack Thompson, an antigaming activist who has brought lawsuits against the makers of violent games. He has called *Grand Theft Auto* a "murder simulator"[2] and argues that it can turn young men into killers.

Indeed, research indicates that video games can affect behavior more profoundly than watching television can. Psychologist Elizabeth Carll explains, "In a game

"In a game . . . if it is killing people that you're doing, you get a reward for that."[3]

— Psychologist Elizabeth Carll.

you do things over and over again, whereas in the movies or on television you watch it once. And in the game there is reinforcement for it. So if it is killing people that you're doing, you get a reward for that."[3]

Racist and Sexist Depictions

Critics of gaming note that murder is not the only kind of bad behavior modeled in violent video games. Some games feature characters who engage in hate crimes or at least make derogatory comments about women and minorities. In fact, according to a study by the advocacy group Children Now, the majority of video games feature heroes who are white, while minorities are often depicted as villains or minor characters.

Many nongamers consider these findings disturbing. They worry that players who take on the role of characters who victimize women and minorities are being encouraged to think like racists, sexists, and homophobes, and that these adopted attitudes might carry over into everyday life. And even if this does not happen, critics say, then gamers might at least become more tolerant of racist, sexist, or homophobic remarks by others, which could ultimately lead to a society where such remarks are considered acceptable.

Video gaming can also damage society, critics say, because of the ways in which it encourages people to lose track of time. Absorbed in the game world, players sometimes forget responsibilities and miss work or school or fail to maintain personal relationships. Ultimately, the most obsessed players can end up having to rely on the resources of others for financial and emotional support, thereby becoming a drain on society rather than an asset.

Benefits

But psychologists and others who have studied the effects of gaming say that when enjoyed in moderation, video games—even violent ones—can have many benefits. For example, when played in concert with others, video games can promote cooperative behavior and help develop social skills. They can also make players better at interpreting, analyzing, and solving problems; multitasking; thinking strategically; formulating and executing plans; and adapting to rapid changes. In order to succeed, game players typically take a trial-and-error approach to their tasks, which makes them active problem solvers who view their mistakes as opportunities to improve. This attitude can help them in everyday life.

Video games can also improve hand-eye coordination. In fact, a study in 2011 reported in the medical journal *Archives of Surgery* found that regularly playing video games can make a surgeon more skilled at laparoscopic surgery, which involves making very tiny incisions. Similarly, the US military has found that video gaming can familiarize new recruits with combat situations and condition them for war by training them to make split-second decisions involving hard choices.

"Hardcore games tend to get the lion's share of publicity."[4]

— Patricia Vance, president of the Entertainment Software Rating Board (ESRB).

Such benefits to society are often overlooked amid criticisms of the gaming industry. Also often overlooked is the fact that many other games on the market have positive content. Nonetheless, Patricia Vance, president of the Entertainment Software Rating Board (ESRB) that oversees and enforces the industry's game rating system, reports, "Hardcore [violent] games tend to get the lion's share of publicity."[4] This publicity flares up every time a crime like Van der Vlis's is committed, whereupon public outrage over the existence of violent video games results in more calls to restrict the sales of such games even as gaming customers are demanding them.

Facts

- In 2010 the average age of American video gamers was thirty, with 53 percent male and 47 percent female.

- Surveys conducted in 2012 indicate that 97 percent of US teens regularly play games via a computer, the Internet, or a gaming console.

- Seventy-eight percent of gamers who played with others during the first half of 2012 did so or at least an hour a week.

- In 2012, 33 percent of videogamers played social games.

- In a survey of gamers during the first half of 2012, 46 percent said they had already purchased or planned to purchase at least one more video game.

What Are the Origins of the Violent Video Game Controversy?

Shortly after 11 a.m. on Tuesday, April 20, 1999, eighteen-year-old Eric Harris and seventeen-year-old Dylan Klebold, both seniors at Columbine High School in Jefferson County, Colorado, left two gym bags containing homemade bombs in their school cafeteria, then went outside to wait in their cars for the explosion. They had timed the bombs to go off at 11:17 a.m., having determined that this was the cafeteria's busiest time, and they hoped the blast would bring down the library above the cafeteria as well.

Harris and Klebold also planned to shoot any blast survivors who ran outside. To this end, they had armed themselves with four knives, two sawed-off shotguns, a rifle, and a semiautomatic pistol. In addition, they had brought with them backpacks and duffle bags filled with explosives and ammunition, ready to be carried inside the building to kill still more people after the initial explosion. Earlier they had placed bombs in a field 3 miles (4.8 km) from the school as well, timed to go off two minutes before the cafeteria bombs as a distraction for police and fire personnel, and they had planted gasoline bombs in their cars, timed to kill any rescue personnel or parents who rushed to the school's parking lot to help the wounded. By that time, Harris and Klebold planned to be inside the school, shooting more students.

At 11:15 a.m., one of the distant bombs went off on schedule, but the others failed to explode. Both bombs in the cafeteria also failed to explode. Frustrated, Harris and Klebold got out of their cars with their weapons and bags, headed to the school, and began firing at people. Twelve students and one teacher died in the massacre, an additional twenty-one people were shot but survived, and three more injured themselves accidentally while escaping the building. Harris and Klebold also attempted to set off more explosives inside the school but failed, and eventually the two committed suicide by shooting themselves.

Motives

As with similar violent events, in the aftermath of the Columbine shootings experts tried to determine the motivations behind the killings. Most experts believe these two young men were psychopaths—individuals with a personality disorder that can lead them to become killers. (Such people have little or no empathy, for example, and are egocentric, both of which mean they do not care about the well-being of others.) But not all psychopaths engage in violent acts, and especially not mass murders. So what might have triggered Harris and Klebold to do this?

One of the first motives that the media cited in the aftermath of the killings was bullying. Unpopular at school, Harris and Klebold had been the victims of significant, frequent bullying since at least the tenth grade, and by the twelfth grade they were bullies themselves, targeting younger students and boys they judged to be homosexual. They had also been in trouble with the law for stealing, and Harris was on a powerful antidepressant and was seeing a psychiatrist.

Another motive was the pair's obsession with violence. The two often talked about guns and explosives, and Harris wrote about them in journals. For school assignments he also created short stories and a video that featured him and Klebold using fake guns to "shoot" students in their school's hallways. Other videos they had made and kept private showed the two practicing shooting in hills near their home, talking about how they obtained and hid their weapons, and discussing the violence they had planned.

Early media reports also blamed the movie *The Matrix*, released just weeks before the killings, because during the massacre Harris and Klebold had been wearing long black coats similar to those worn by *Matrix* characters who "shot" people. But as more information became available about the killers' lives, the media shifted its blame to a violent video game called *Doom*. In early 1996 Harris had created a private *Doom*-related website where he could host people who wanted to play levels of the game that he and Klebold had created, and he used it as a place to blog about his collection of guns, his bomb-building efforts, and his desire to kill people. In other writings, Harris compared his plans for the massacre to aspects of *Doom*, as well as to another video game called *Duke Nukem*, and he said that he had chosen his shotgun because it was essentially the same as a weapon in *Doom*.

The *Doom* Shooter

First made available to the public in December 1993, *Doom* is particularly significant in the history of violent video games not only because of its connection to the Columbine killings but also because it popularized the first-person shooter approach to gaming. This means that the game is played from the perspective of a character who is shooting enemies, so that the player watches through the eyes of that character as victims die, usually in gruesome ways. A game released the previous year, *Mortal Kombat*, was actually the first to put the player in the skin of a killer—who destroyed enemies through hand-to-hand combat, decapitation, and the ripping out of hearts—but at that point it was an arcade game. As a game made for personal computers, *Doom* brought its graphic violence into the home.

Doom was also a pioneer in regard to the level of realism in video games. Played from the perspective of a marine at a military

base on a moon of Mars who must shoot and kill invading demons from hell, the game features graphics that were advanced for their time, simulating a 3-D experience in order to completely immerse players in the game environment. As a result, *Doom*'s violence is both graphic and interactive. It also provides such realistic gameplay that shortly after its release, the US Marine Corps ordered some of its members to play the game in order to hone their reflexes as part of urban warfare training.

Death Race

Parents were less enthusiastic than the military about *Doom*'s release. In fact, the game's gory kill simulations triggered widespread criticism among the general public. This public outcry, coupled with the game's subsequent connection to the Columbine killings, has led to the common misperception today that *Doom*'s creation marks the beginning of the controversy over violence in video

A video shot for a class project shows trench coat-clad Eric Harris (left) and Dylan Klebold (right) walking in a hallway at Columbine High School. The two teens later killed thirteen people and injured many others at the school. The shooting has been linked to at least two violent video games.

games. However, people began complaining about the violence in video games as early as the 1970s.

Perhaps the biggest target of such complaints was the 1976 arcade game *Death Race*, inspired by a 1975 movie of the same name. The point of the game was to run over fleeing gremlins with cars, and although the game's graphics were far from realistic, parents complained that it encouraged violence against pedestrians because the gremlins seemed more like humans than otherworldly beings. (Indeed, prior to its release the game's title was *Pedestrian*.) Eddie Adlum, publisher of the gaming magazine *RePlay*, reports, "It's very tame by today's standards. Every time you made a hit, a little cross would appear on the monitor signifying a grave. Nice

Spacewar!

Shooting at enemies has been a part of gaming ever since the first video games were created. One of the earliest known examples of such games, *Spacewar!* (1961), required two players to fire at each other's armed spaceships even as a star in the center of the screen threatened to pull both ships into it. The game also had a hyperspace feature that allowed players to escape disaster by jumping to another spot on the screen, but if used too often this feature could cause a ship to explode.

Spacewar! was extremely primitive by today's standards. Its graphics were simply white spots of light against a black background on a small screen, and the blips of light representing the ships were not much bigger than the blips representing the blasts they fired. Nonetheless, it took developer Steve Russell, a computer engineering student at the Massachusetts Institute of Technology (MIT) nearly six months to develop the game. Undoubtedly he never imagined just how sophisticated video game space battles of the future would be.

game. Fun. Bottom line, the game really took off when TV stations started to get some complaints from irate parents that this was a terrible example to set for children. The industry got a lot of coast-to-coast coverage during news programs."[5]

Organizations like the National Safety Council also condemned the game, and some stores stopped selling *Death Race* because of the negative media attention.

Violence Expands

Despite the outcry, the 1980s saw an increase in game violence. One of the most notorious games of this period was *Custer's Revenge* (1983), in which a figure representing Indian fighter General George Custer would, if he could dodge arrows to get to her, rape a bound Native American girl. Not only parents but civil rights groups protested this game, including an organization called Women Against Pornography whose members picketed places where *Custer's Revenge* was sold. However, the resulting media attention only made people curious about the game, and sales rose. In fact, some gaming experts believe that the publicity more than doubled the game's sales.

The introduction of the Sony PlayStation in the 1980s triggered numerous complaints as well because the device allowed for more realistic violence. Government officials also expressed concern about violence in video games during this period. For example, in 1983 the surgeon general of the United States, C. Everett Koop, gave a speech in which he warned that gaming could be highly addictive and speculated that violent games could encourage players to act in violent ways outside of the game environment. Of gamers he said, "They are into it body and soul. There's nothing constructive in the games. Everything is eliminate, kill, destroy and do it fast."[6]

"Everything is eliminate, kill, destroy and do it fast."[6]

— C. Everett Koop, former US surgeon general.

Duke Nukem

In the 1990s the connection between the Columbine killings and the game *Doom* confirmed peoples' fears that game violence could lead to real-life violence. By this time the makers of *Doom*, id Software, had created several sequels and expansion packs to the still-popular game, including *Doom II* (1994), *The Ultimate Doom* (1995), and *Final Doom* (1996). During the same period, other software developers adopted the first-person shooter approach to gaming as well, producing games that were commonly referred to as *Doom* clones. These include *Duke Nukem 3D* (1994), the game Harris referred to in his journals in addition to *Doom*.

In the wake of Columbine, the *Duke Nukem* series received the same criticism as *Doom* in regard to violence. But it was also criticized for its coupling of violence with sex and its depictions of women. While acting as the first-person shooter, players of *Duke Nukem 3D* sometimes kill women who have been tied up, sometimes half naked, and the game also includes depictions of prostitutes, strippers, and pornography shops. Most players have no problem with these features. In fact, some feel they add spice to the game. For example, in reflecting on *Duke Nukem 3D*'s strong points, Ben Kuchera, a reviewer in the online magazine *Ars Technica*, says, "The game rewarded you for exploring, and the shooting itself was satisfying. The whole experience had little padding to it, and the "mature" elements of the game added flavor to what was already a wonderful game. If impressive level design was the cake, paying strippers was the icing."[7]

Topping Previous Levels

Given such praise and robust sales, *Duke Nukem 3D*'s creators did not allow complaints by parents, psychologists, and others to deter them from including the same kind of content in the next game in the series, *Duke Nukem Forever* (2011). In fact, they made this version even more extreme in terms of sex and violence and crude, vulgar, sexist, and racist remarks. As a result, even some fans of *Duke Nukem 3D* criticized *Duke Nukem Forever*. For example, Kuchera calls the game "barely playable, not funny, [and] rampantly offensive" and adds, "Every time I put the controller down, I felt the need to rub my hands on my jeans as if the game were making me physically dirty. It's like watching your uncle tell racist jokes at Thanksgiving and praying someone has the guts to tell him to cut it out, but this time it's interactive—and you're the uncle."[8]

In exceeding previous levels of violence and sexism, the creators of *Duke Nukem Forever* could be said to be following a tradition in the gaming industry: that of new games trying to top whatever came before. Most software designers embrace the notion that every new entry into the gaming marketplace should be more technologically advanced than its predecessors, and some apply this can-you-top-this approach to levels of sex and violence as well, especially where series are concerned. The result is that with each passing year, games get more and more violent, and critics say that the boundary between acceptable and unacceptable violence has been crossed.

People disagree on when this began to be common practice, but many cite *Mortal Kombat* as the game that launched software developers on a path of gore and more gore. Jeffrey L. Wilson of *PC Magazine* explains:

> Over the years, there have been, admittedly, several titles in the [gaming] hobby's relatively brief history that have pushed the boundaries of decency in many critics' eyes. Mortal Kombat, Midway Games' blood-fest, is the granddaddy of violent video games with its graphic displays of decapitations, beheadings, and other over-the-top carnage. And when Mortal Kombat opened that door, the chainsaws, shotguns, cleavers, and other instruments of death . . . rushed through.[9]

"It's like watching your uncle tell racist jokes at Thanksgiving and praying someone has the guts to tell him to cut it out, but this time it's interactive— and you're the uncle."[8]

— Ben Kuchera, in his review of *Duke Nukem Forever*.

Wilson cites ten games as being the most violent in gaming history as of June 2012. In addition to the 2011 version of *Mortal Kombat*, which includes an X-ray feature that allows players to view the internal damage in the bodies of characters being killed, he names two other games that have received a great deal of media attention for their violence: *Call of Duty: Modern Warfare 2* (2010) and *Grand Theft Auto III* (2011). Wilson also names *Deadspace* (2008) for the way it gruesomely uses mining tools as weapons; *God of War III* (2010) for showing decapitation, impalement, and limb removal; *Soldier of Fortune* (2000) for its disembowelments and explosions of body parts; *Splatterhouse* (2010) for its copious

A gamer attending a convention snaps a photo of a scene from the video game Doom.

amounts of splattered blood, *MadWorld* (2009) for graphic chain-saw deaths; *Postal* (1997), which shows the suffering of innocent victims who have been shot, and *Manhunt* (2003), which gives players more points for more-brutal killings.

Attracting Publicity

But whereas some people complain about violent games like those on Wilson's list, others seek them out, believing that violence makes a game better. For example, in reviewing *Killer7* (2005), in which first-person shooters collect their victims' blood and must slit their own wrists to spray blood at certain points in the game, Tom Orry of Videogamer, an online gamers' site, complains about times in the game when victims are felled with just one shot. He says that "the annoyance factor kicks in" whenever there are cases of "one-hit deaths happening far too frequently and a number of cheap in-your-face [enemies] taking you out before you have the chance to draw your weapon."[10]

Because of attitudes like this, some game developers have decided to publicize their games' violence to attract buyers. This appears to be the case, for example, with the 2003 release of *Postal 2*. The game's developers included features that seemed designed to attract publicity by inciting criticism, which they dismissed by saying it was the players' choice whether to engage in the game's violent acts. Doug Gross, who reports on video games for the CNN Tech website, explains:

> While other game creators try to reflect or explain away criticism, the makers of the "Postal" franchise have wallowed in it. To be honest, their offering is pretty much what the harshest critics see in their heads when they imagine violent video games. Abusing and killing cats. Killing people who cut ahead of you in line at the bank. . . . All are allowed, and much more. (And if you forget exactly how much your character has . . . [done,] don't worry. Its scoring system will keep track for you . . . [with] stats like "Number of People Murdered," "People Roasted" and "Heads Exploded by Shotgun"). In a move that probably seemed clever to someone, you can even kill people protesting against violent video games. Get it?[11]

For their efforts, the makers of the game were rewarded with sales strong enough to support a sequel, *Postal III* (2011), even though *Postal 2* received many bad reviews. Well-reviewed violent video games enjoy even more success. For example, the critically acclaimed 2004 game *Grand Theft Auto: San Andreas* was the highest-selling game for the gaming system PlayStation 2, as well as the third best-selling game of all time as of 2010. And yet the Common Sense Media website says the game "is raunchy and violent and portrays just about every deviant act that a criminal could think of in full, living 3-D graphics."[12] The game includes racial stereotyping and violence against women as well.

Hidden Content

Grand Theft Auto: San Andreas has also received a great deal of criticism for its hidden sexual content. Upon its release, the Microsoft

Grand Theft Auto, Driving Teacher

People who believe video games can adversely influence young people often cite a January 2009 incident in Virginia as proof that they are right. This incident involved a six-year-old boy who missed his school bus and decided to drive himself to school rather than bother his sleeping mother. After taking the keys for the family's Ford Taurus, he drove nearly six miles on a two-lane road, passing several cars along the way. As part of his drive he successfully made at least two ninety-degree turns, but he also ran off the road several times. About a mile and a half from his destination, he hit an embankment and crashed the car into a utility pole, receiving minor injuries. He then tried to walk the rest of the way to school. He later told police that he had learned to drive by playing *Grand Theft Auto* and *Monster Truck Jam* video games.

Windows version of the game included sex scenes that could be accessed via an easily downloaded software patch that unlocked these scenes. After the media reported on this secret content, the resulting outcry led Rockstar Games, which created the game, to recall existing copies and replace them with ones that did not have the sexually explicit content.

By this time, however, hackers had discovered that the sex scenes could also be accessed through PlayStation 2 and Xbox versions of the game. Meanwhile lawmakers were demanding that the game be relabeled as being for adults only. To avoid this relabeling—which could have reduced sales and therefore profits—Rockstar Games released a new version without the hidden content, as well as a patch that would crash the original version of game if anyone tried to access its sexual content.

In the wake of this incident, the video game industry sought to protect itself from future condemnation over the hidden content issue. Specifically, the industry's Entertainment Software Rating Board (ESRB), which rates games in order to guide parents in selecting appropriate content for children, notified all game developers that hidden content would be taken into account when rating games, not just in the future but retroactively. Its notification states:

> Coding around scenes, images, or similar elements that might be pertinent to a rating assignment does not render this content irrelevant from a ratings standpoint. If a publisher wishes to "edit out" pertinent content from a final product, it must remove the content from the disc altogether. If that is not feasible, the pertinent content must be disclosed to the ESRB during the rating process so it can be taken into account in the assignment of a rating.[13]

Avoiding Restrictions

In responding so quickly and firmly to the controversy, the gaming industry wanted to ensure that its game ratings remained voluntary rather than mandated by law. This is because many in the industry believe that such a mandate might lead to restrictions on game content, and game developers want to continue to have the right to express themselves however they like. Similarly, gamers believe they should have the same right to play whatever kind of game they want—especially since people disagree on whether violent games can inspire anyone to commit violent acts.

In fact, some people believe that it is wrong even to suggest a connection between violent video games and shootings like those at Columbine. Such events, they argue, are the result solely of a defect within the mind of the killers. For example, in speaking of Harris and Klebold, psychologist Peter Langman, author of the book *Why Kids Kill: Inside the Minds of School Shooters*, says: "These are not ordinary kids who were bullied into retaliation. These are not ordinary kids who played too many video games. These are not ordinary kids who just wanted to be famous. These are simply *not ordinary kids*. These are kids with serious psychological problems."[14]

Others have noted that when the media finds a connection, no matter how weak, between a crime and a particular video game, reporters leap to blame the game for the crime. Journalist Brian Ashcraft sums up this trend by saying, "Video games have been scapegoats. Need something to blame social problems on? Blame video games."[15]

Ashcraft scoffs at this tendency to blame video games. Those who see a cause-and-effect relationship between gaming violence and real violence, however, insist the blame is warranted. Meanwhile, game developers who keep pushing the envelope in regard to the amount of violence, sex, and offensive language they offer to gamers are ensuring that the controversy over these games will continue for the foreseeable future.

Facts

- The first commercially successful video game, *Pong* (1972), was a version of table tennis in which two players "hit" a virtual ball back and forth.

- Until Atari released a home version of a gaming console in 1977, video games could only be played on a coin-operated machine usually housed in an arcade.

- During the 1980s parents publicly protested against locating game arcades near elementary schools because of concerns that violent video games might encourage schoolyard violence.

- The 1974 video game *Maze Wars* is generally considered the predecessor of all first-person shooter games because players—represented as eyeballs—viewed the playing field, a maze, as though they were actually inside of it.

- *Galaxy Game*, the earliest known coin-operated video arcade game, was first installed in September 1971 at Stanford University in the student union; the game cost ten cents to play, or three games for twenty-five cents.

Do Violent Video Games Encourage Violent Acts?

On July 22, 2011, thirty-two-year-old Anders Behring Breivik of Oslo, Norway, donned a police uniform and a face-concealing police helmet and got into a Volkswagen van containing a bomb he had made from fuel oil and a fertilizer that could produce an explosive gas. Breivik drove the van to central Oslo, parked it in front of a seventeen-story government building that included the Norwegian prime minister's office, and left the area. The bomb subsequently exploded, killing eight people and injuring over two hundred, though not the prime minister.

At this point Breivik was already focused on his next target: a political summer camp on the island of Utøya, roughly twenty-five miles from Oslo. Hosted annually by the youth division of the Norweigian Labour Party, then in control of Norway's government, the camp held approximately six hundred teens, many of them the children of political leaders. After Breivik arrived there by ferry, still in his uniform and carrying a bag filled with weapons and ammunition, he told both a camp leader and a security officer that he had been sent by the police department to check on the young people's safety. Then he shot both of them and began firing at teens.

School Shooter Game

In March 2011 a game-hosting site on the Internet pulled the game *School Shooter: North American Tour 2012* from its database because of controversy over its content. Specifically, this game, a modification of an existing popular game called *Half-Life 2*, would have allowed players to shoot students in a setting where an actual school shooting took place: Columbine High School. Players would use the same weapons as the Columbine shooters and would be encouraged to kill themselves at the end of the virtual shooting spree, just as the killers did in real life. In response to the controversy over *School Shooter*, game developer Jaime Lombe, also known as Pawnstick, told reporters that he did not understand the objections, adding that he just wanted to create a good school shooting game.

For roughly an hour and a half he continued shooting people as they ran, including those who dived into the water to escape him. He also returned to some of the wounded to kill them. A few of the young people armed themselves with rocks, intending to try to stop the gunman, but as they crept up on him they grew too scared and ran to hide. Others were already hiding in caves and buildings on the island, or they were lying on the ground pretending to be dead. Meanwhile, some vacationers in the area managed to pilot their boats to rescue people from the water while Breivik was shooting elsewhere, and an additional 150 or so of the teens managed to swim to the opposite shore for safety. Nonetheless, Breivik still managed to kill 69 and injure 66 before police arrived and he surrendered to them.

Motives

As with other mass shootings, the aftermath of the event involved much speculation as to why Breivik did what he did. Fortunately for investigators, he left writings to explain his motives, including a manifesto connecting his political beliefs to his terrorist attacks. Breivik was a right-wing Christian fundamentalist extremist who claimed to be a member of a group whose goal was to seize control of governments in western Europe. The group's ultimate purpose, he said, was to fight multiculturalism and immigration in order to defend the Christian world from Muslims. (Investigators later concluded that Breivik had actually acted alone.)

Breivik believed that violence was the only way to achieve his aims. He stated, "The time for dialogue is over. We gave peace a chance. The time for armed resistance has come."[16] He had also previously been involved in anti-tax, anti-immigrant, and anti-Muslim activism, and he had been planning terrorist attacks for months.

Call of Duty: Modern Warfare 2

Clearly, then, Breivik's violent acts were based on his political beliefs. But Breivik's testimony during his trial for the murders pointed to a video game connection as well. He had spent many hours playing the video game *Call of Duty: Modern Warfare 2* and had incorporated some of its details into his plans.

Specifically, Breivik testified that *Call of Duty: Modern Warfare 2* gave him the idea to equip his weapon with a holographic sight, because this is what the game's first-person shooters use. He further testified that had it not been for the holographic sight, he might not have been able to kill so many people, explaining, "If you are familiar with a holographic sight, it's built up in such a way that you could have given it to your grandmother and she would have been a super marksman. It's designed to be used by anyone. In reality it requires very little training to use it in an optimal way. But of course it does help if you've practiced using a simulator [like *Call of Duty: Modern Warfare 2*]."[17]

Cooperative Gaming

Breivik also testified that he had played another video game, *World of Warcraft 2*, for many hours but said this game had no bearing on the shootings because it is "only a fantasy game, which is not violent at all. . . . It's a strategy game. You co-operate with a lot of others to overcome challenges. . . . It's a very social game." In contrast,

Anders Behring Breivik appears in court in 2012 in Oslo, Norway. The right-wing extremist is accused of killing and injuring dozens at a youth summer camp. In testimony, Breivik talked about the video games that influenced his actions.

he said that a first-person shooter game "consists of many hundreds of different tasks [involved with killing people] and some of these tasks can be compared with an attack, for real."[18]

While Breivik is incorrect when he says that *World of Warcraft* is not violent, most people familiar with the game would agree that its violence is not in the same league as *Call of Duty: Modern Warfare 2*. An online role-playing game that can involve millions of players across the Internet, *World of Warcraft* features quests and battles during which characters—including fantasy beings like trolls, gnomes, and elves, controlled either by the game's software or by other players—can get killed, but no blood or gore is associated with these deaths. It is also a cooperative game, as Breivik correctly noted. Participants must play for either the Horde faction or the Alliance faction, and the game will not let them kill a character from their own faction.

Because of these features Wendy Kays, a frequent critic of video games and the author of a book on gaming called *Game*

Widow, believes that *World of Warcraft* is far more about achieving things than killing things. She explains, "Despite the fact that you're in combat for a lot of the time, the point of WoW [*World of Warcraft*] isn't killing. It's just a safe way to explore new things, an inexpensive way to feel as if you're being a pioneer. It's emotionally compelling—and I have to say that while researching the game I ended up loving it."[19]

Scapegoats

Nonetheless, after Breivik's testimony, many in the media condemned *World of Warcraft*, suggesting it was as violent as *Call of Duty: Modern Warfare 2*. For example, CNN editorialist Andrew Keen writes:

> Most troubling of all is Breivik's obsession with the multiplayer role-playing *World of Warcraft*, a violent online game. . . . Some apologists for video games have suggested that Breivik's addiction to *World of Warcraft* 'means nothing at all.' But they are wrong. Given his absolute absence of remorse over the murders, it's not hard to imagine that this obsession with violent online games has enabled him to somehow virtualize the killing of real people, transforming them from flesh and blood characters into abstractions.[20]

Keen labels Breivik's *World of Warcraft* play as "most troubling" even after listing a host of other, seemingly more troubling things about the killer, including the possibility that he is criminally insane. This is the kind of media response that frustrates experts on video gaming. For example, in the aftermath of the Breivik shooting, Matt Peckham of *Time* magazine complained about the media's kneejerk connection between the deaths and *World of Warcraft*. He says, "We're likely to hear plenty more about World of Warcraft and Breivik's yearlong video-game-playing spree by news networks that understand perfectly well the hunger for cause-and-effect explanations, or barring that, a flat-out scapegoat."[21]

Peckham believes that when people are assessing blame, the best scapegoat is the unfamiliar, the strange—something we do not understand and therefore might be afraid of anyway. He explains:

When horrible things happen, we look for simple answers, for easy rationalizations—ways to essentially say, Oh, this is why so-and-so did such-and-such. We want the "why" right now, when the spotlight's on. We want the dots connected, and we want them to correspond with our suspicions about new, ultra-popular activities, like dancing to jazz music in the 1920s, or reading comics in the 1950s, or listening to rock 'n' roll in the 1960s, or playing Dungeons & Dragons in the 1980s—or playing violent video games pretty much from the 1990s on.[22]

Causing Violence?

Many gaming experts do not believe that violent video games cause killing sprees. For example, Paul Tassi says, "The media just refuses to let the notion go that video games somehow create violence, even though it's never been scientifically proven and 99.99999% of gamers who even play the most gruesome of titles do not end up killing anyone, much less 77 people."[23] Moreover, Christopher J. Ferguson, associate professor of psychology and criminal justice at Texas A&M International University, reports that "even while video game sales have skyrocketed, youth violence plummeted to its lowest levels in 40 years according to government statistics."[24]

Ferguson also reports that while early studies suggested a possible connection between violence in games and violent acts committed by gamers, recent research does not bear this out. Those early studies seemed to show that playing violent video games makes young people more aggressive. But according to Ferguson, the studies "failed to control carefully for other important variables, such as family violence, mental health issues or even gender in many studies (boys play more VVG [violent video games] and are more aggressive [generally than girls]."[25] For this reason, the US Supreme Court specifically rejected these studies when considering in 2011 whether to ban the sale of violent video games to minors.

Ferguson himself has conducted a three-year study of the effect

"When horrible things happen, we look for simple answers, for easy rationalizations—ways to essentially say, Oh, this is why so-and-so did such-and-such."[22]

— Matt Peckham of *Time* magazine.

of violent games on children aged ten to fourteen and has found no link between violent video games and either aggression or dating violence in young people. Another recent study in Germany also found no such links. Additional research has suggested another reason for early findings that gamers became more aggressive after playing violent video games: Players were not given enough time to become familiar with the game. That is, the duration of play was so short that players left the game frustrated because they were unable to perform well, and in acting out this frustration they exhibited more aggression than normal. Ferguson reports:

> Since . . . violent games tend to be more difficult to learn and have more complex controls than non-violent games, it appears that many participants in these experiments may simply have been frustrated by being cut off so quickly before they even learned how to play, rather than by the violent content of the game. Letting them play long enough to learn the game, or simply providing violent and non-violent games of equal complexity, erases the effects. In fact, experimental research led by my graduate student Jose Valadez found that both violent and non-violent games tend to relax people over time, not anger them.[26]

Cause Versus Influence

Even if violent gaming did not cause the Norway massacre, it does seem to have influenced it. Breivik himself acknowledges that *Call of Duty: Modern Warfare 2* affected his decisions and actions prior to and during the attack. In a diary entry from February 2010 he calls *Modern Warfare 2* "the best military simulator out there," adding, "I see MW2 more as a part of my training-simulation than anything else. . . . You can more or less completely simulate actual operations."[27]

Some gaming experts disagree with the notion that someone could learn real-life military skills just from playing a game. For example, Tassi says that "being good at Call of Duty makes you about as competent a soldier as playing Dr. Mario makes you a cardiovascular surgeon."[28] But Jack Thompson would disagree. He has sued game makers and marketers on behalf of the families of gamers who

Halo 3 Shooting

A sixteen-year-old from a strict religious household in Ohio, Daniel Petric was introduced to the first-person shooter game *Halo 3* while at a friend's house in September 2007. He enjoyed it so much he wanted his own copy of the newly released game, but his parents not only refused to let him have one but told him he could never play the game again. Shortly thereafter he sneaked out of the house to buy it for himself, and he secretly played the game for many hours before his parents found out, took it away, and locked it in their gun safe. A month later Petric stole the key to the safe, intending to simply retrieve the game. When he saw the gun, however, he decided to shoot his parents, too. He fired at them from behind several times, killing his mother and seriously wounding his father before being interrupted by the arrival of his sister and her husband. They immediately called for help, and when the police arrived they found Petric playing *Halo 3*. The following year he was sentenced to twenty-three years in prison.

committed murder, arguing in essence that without the skills and attitude they acquired through gaming they would not have killed.

One of Thompson's most prominent cases was that of Alabama teenager Devin Moore, who shot a police dispatcher and two policemen after he was brought to the police station under suspicion of stealing a car. Afraid of going to jail, Moore grabbed the gun of one of the policemen and went on a shooting rampage before stealing a car and fleeing. Prior to this incident Moore had no history of breaking the law, but he had spent many hours playing *Grand Theft Auto: Vice City*, in which players kill policemen. Consequently Thompson believes that this video game taught Moore to react the way he did around police. He says, "Devin Moore was, in effect, trained to do what he did. He was given a murder simulator.

. . . He bought it as a minor. He played it hundreds of hours, which is primarily a cop-killing game. It's our theory . . . that, but for the video-game training, he would not have done what he did."[29]

Thompson was unsuccessful in convincing a judge that video games were to blame for Moore's murders. Nonetheless, he remains insistent that gaming provided Moore with the mindset to kill. He and others believe Moore had no aversion to killing police because he was accustomed to doing it in the game.

In the case of the Norway massacre, Breivik's mind also seems to have been affected by his exposure to gaming, given the language in his writings. As Tom Law, a writer who provides dialogue for video games, notes, "His writing often feels more like an instruction manual for a game than a terrorist manifesto. There are rules to learn, ranks to 'level-up' through, scenarios to complete and medals to unlock."[30]

Training Killers

Some antigaming experts argue that this mindset is part of a conditioning process whereby gamers are taught to become killers.

One of the video games mentioned in connection with several high-profile shootings is Call of Duty: Modern Warfare 2 *(pictured). Some experts say that such games encourage aggressive and violent behavior but others say most teens understand the difference between games and real life.*

One of the leading proponents of this idea is Dave Grossman, a retired lieutenant colonel in the US Army and former teacher of psychology at the United States Military Academy at West Point. Grossman argues that playing violent video games desensitizes players to violence, thereby hardening their emotions to the point where they can kill in real life.

Grossman believes that children are being conditioned to engage in violent acts by being rewarded during game play for every violent act they commit. As a result, he says, "Our kids are learning to kill and learning to like it."[31] He says that this conditioning will persist and affect their actions in the real world, arguing that "by sitting and mindlessly killing countless thousands of fellow members of your own species without any ramification or repercussions, we are teaching skills and concepts and values that transfer immediately anytime they get a real weapon in their hand."[32]

Improving Accuracy

Grossman's position that video games are conditioning kids to become killers has many detractors. Another of his arguments against violent video games, however, is more accepted: that first-person shooter games make people who play such games more lethal by improving their ability to accurately aim and shoot real guns. In support of this belief, Grossman cites a school shooting case in Paducah, Kentucky, involving a fourteen-year-old boy who shot at eight children and hit all of them, five in the head and three in the upper torso. About this shooting feat Grossman says, "I train numerous elite military and law enforcement organizations around the world. When I tell them of this achievement they are stunned. Nowhere in the annals of military or law enforcement history can we find an equivalent 'achievement.' Where does a 14-year-old boy who never fired a gun before get the skill and the will to kill? Video games and media violence."[33]

Indeed, the military, police departments, and other law enforcement agencies use video games as a way to improve people's shooting skills, and studies have shown that practicing with virtual guns can improve even a civilian's accuracy with real guns. In fact, in one recent study conducted at Ohio State University, just twenty minutes of playing a first-person shooter game made college students more accurate when shooting at a mannequin. It also made study participants much more likely to fire at the mannequin's head than at the torso. Coauthor of the study Brad Bushman, a professor of communication and psychology, concludes, "For good and bad, video game players are learning lessons that can be applied in the real world."[34]

Bushman stresses that he is not saying such games encourage people to commit real-life acts of violence. It was not his study's purpose to determine whether such a cause-and-effect relationship exists. "But," he says, "this study suggests these games can teach people to shoot more accurately and aim to the head," and therefore "we shouldn't be too quick to dismiss violent video games as just harmless fun in a fantasy world."[35]

A US soldier trains for urban warfare with the help of a video game. Training of this sort is being used more and more by law enforcement and the military.

Reality Versus Fantasy

People who see no harm in violent video games often dismiss others' concerns by saying that such games are clearly fantasy. But

distinguishing between fantasy and reality is not always that clear cut. Grossman, for example, reports that up until the age of six or seven, children cannot tell the difference between fantasy and reality, and he argues that if they are overexposed to violence during this formative period, they will continue to blur the lines between fantasy and reality into adulthood. He says, "The Holy Grail of this industry is realism, seeking ever greater levels of realism. And, when the child spends more waking hours playing the game than he does anything else, what becomes fantasy and what becomes reality?"[36]

But Henry Jenkins, a director of comparative studies at MIT, counters that studies do not bear out this position. In fact, he reports that even primates know the difference between violence associated with games and violence associated with real battles. He says, "Classic studies of play behavior among primates suggest that apes make basic distinctions between play fighting and actual combat. In some circumstances, they seem to take pleasure wrestling and tousling with each other. In others, they might rip each other apart in mortal combat. . . . [For humans] the same action—say, sweeping a floor—may take on different meanings in play (as in playing house) than in reality (housework)."[37]

However, critics of violent video games question why these games have to be so realistic if they are meant to represent fantasies. Why make it so easy to blur fantasy and reality, they ask, if there is even a slight risk that someone might die because a gamer cannot make the distinction? Why give disturbed people a way to act out fantasies of killing that they might eventually decide to make a reality? Surely, critics say, features like cop killing and shooting innocent civilians who scream as they die are not necessary for game enjoyment.

One of those questioning the rationale for making games with these features is Steve Strickland, brother of one of the policemen murdered by Moore. He says, "The question I have to ask the manufacturers of them is, 'Why do you make games that target people that are to protect us, police officers, people that we look

"When the child spends more waking hours playing the game than he does anything else, what becomes fantasy and what becomes reality?"[36]

— Dave Grossman, expert on gaming violence.

up to . . . Why do you want to market a game that gives people the thoughts, even the thoughts of thinking it's OK to shoot police officers?'"[38] But people who enjoy such games argue that virtual shooting and real shooting are not the same thing, and that a game cannot give them the idea to kill a living person.

Facts

- During the first twenty-four hours of sales, *Call of Duty: Modern Warfare 2* brought in $310 million in the United States and UK; after five days, $550 million worldwide; and as of January 2010, over $1 billion worldwide.

- As of November 2011 the US military had formally adapted more than twenty-three video games as training programs.

- The US military has called for game designers to come up with ways to add an impulse force to their games so that players will feel like they have been hit by bomb debris or bullets during play, thereby becoming conditioned for the pain of war.

- In October 2011, Rockstar Games, the company behind the *Grand Theft Auto* game series, announced that it would not be developing any first-person shooter games because that is not the type of game the leaders of the company prefer to play.

- Communications experts who study the media have noted that in the United States sexual content in video games generates more public controversy than violent content.

Do Violent Video Games Promote Antisocial Behavior?

In November 2011 the news that video gaming company Rockstar Games might be creating a new *Bully* game caused a stir. Gamers greeted this news with excitement because the original *Bully* (2006) and a rereleased variation, *Bully: Scholarship Edition* (2008), had received positive reviews from players. However, parent groups reacted to the news of another *Bully* with dismay because of the controversy surrounding its first two incarnations.

As its title suggests, *Bully* is a game centering around bullying; its main character is teenager Jimmy Hopkins, who must deal with bullies and cliques in a new school. Jimmy "takes crap from no one," according to the game review website Gamefaqs.com, but players have some leeway in deciding how to make Jimmy act within the parameters of the character. "You have the ability to break into lockers, and steal items," Gamefaqs.com reports. "You can throw people into lockers or in trash cans. You can even shove a person's face in a toilet. You can either choose to be an aggressive bully, become a popular jackass, or a respectful person who is most known for being powerful."[39]

Jimmy also pulls pranks and picks up skills, such as learning in chemistry class how to create minor explosions, and he acquires items like baseball bats that can be used as weapons. However, the game penalizes players if they have Jimmy use these weapons against weaker students; Jimmy is supposed to protect the victims of bullies, not victimize them, although he can act like a bully himself in order to punish and humiliate the "bad guys" in the school. Consequently Rockstar Games says: "It is not a game about playing a bully. It is about the trials and tribulations of a boy in his first year at school. He protects children against other characters. People have to be able to make their own decisions and to judge for themselves, with an open mind."[40]

Bad Behavior

Nonetheless, parents began condemning *Bully* even before it was released. Many did so based on the title alone, under the impression that the game would involve the same level of violence as another Rockstar game, *Grand Theft Auto*. But even after parents discovered that *Bully* contains no blood and gore, the criticism continued, in large part because critics felt the game applauded bad behavior by presenting the main character—who, among other things, can set off firecrackers, give wedgies, and beat up bullies—as someone to root for. For example, Niall Cowley of the organization BeatBullying says, "We're disappointed this game was created in the first place. . . . Our philosophy is about educating young people that bullying is not a cool thing to do, and this leaves us with a bad taste in the mouth."[41]

Experts in school violence are also dismayed that Jimmy typically meets bullying with bullying. Psychologist Len Gignac has called this aspect of the game disturbing, adding, "There is good assertive behavior [to prevent becoming a victim of bullies] and there's a big difference between that and bullying back."[42] In addition, critics say the game presents a bad message: that kids who are being bullied should handle the problem themselves rather than telling an adult about it.

Us Versus Them

Critics of *Bully* have also condemned the game for lumping people into categories such as bullies, jocks, geeks, greasers, and preps.

Studies show that violent video games such as Halo 3 *(pictured) might make a person less likely to feel shock when witnessing violence or bad behavior in real life. Violent movies and television programs can have the same effect.*

Players' choices are made based on these categories, and characters act as representatives of their group rather than as individuals. Kristin Kaining, Games editor with MSNBC, explains, "If you choose to defend the geeks, they'll have your back if you run afoul of the jocks. If you team up with the bullies, you might find yourself at a disadvantage with the preps."[43]

Many psychologists believe that this type of labeling and depersonalizing is bad for society, creating barriers between different types of people and making it harder for individuals to empathize with members of groups other than their own. A lack of empathy can also make it easier for people to commit acts of violence against members of other groups. As Greg Lubimiv, executive director of the Phoenix Centre, an antiviolence organization, says in criticizing *Bully*, "If you can't empathize with someone else then it makes it easier to harm others and engage in other anti-social behavior."[44]

While experts in human behavior generally agree that people who lack empathy can find it easier to hurt others, they disagree on whether a video game can cause this inability to understand another person's situation, feelings, and motives. In fact, since a lack of empathy is often a warning sign that a serious mental illness is present, some psychologists doubt that any video game could cause this degree of psychological harm. Therefore if a gamer exhibits a lack of empathy, some experts say, this means that the lack of empathy existed prior to the gaming, and the gaming is only bringing attention to an existing illness. Henry Jenkins, who supports this position, says, "Media reformers argue that playing violent video games can cause a lack of empathy for real-world victims. Yet, a child who responds to a video game the same way he or she responds to a real-world tragedy could be showing symptoms of being severely emotionally disturbed."[45]

Gamers also note that empathy is a big part of games that put players in the skin of a first-person shooter, who might be either a hero or a bad guy. Therefore, as game designer Ken Levine says, "empathy for the characters is something first person shooters need."[46] Some games can also model empathy for players by featuring game characters who show concern for one another. For example, in reviewing the first-person shooter game *Half-Life 2* (2004), Video game blogger and online magazine columnist Michael Abbott praises the way the game builds an "empathetic framework" and notes that one of the characters in this game, Alyx Vance, demonstrates empathy to such a degree that "if you want to know what empathy in video games looks like, you need go no further than her."[47]

> "A child who responds to a video game the same way he or she responds to a real-world tragedy could be showing symptoms of being severely emotionally disturbed."[45]
>
> — Henry Jenkins of MIT.

Desensitization

Abbott, then, believes that some violent video games can encourage empathy. Others disagree. But many people on both sides of this issue concur that violent video games can desensitize players to real-life violent and criminal behavior. That is, the more times a person sees scenes of bad behavior within a game, the less likely the person is to be shocked while witnessing real-life bad behavior. Numerous studies have confirmed this, some by monitoring heart rate and galvanic skin responses (changes in the electrical resistance of the skin, an indication of emotional arousal) to measure a

Affecting Social Behavior

Recent studies have examined whether social behavior can be affected by video gaming. In 2012, for example, psychologists at Iowa State University compared the effect of three types of video games on children aged nine to fourteen: prosocial games (nonviolent games in which characters help one another), neutral games such as pinball, and violent video games. To test the tendency to be helpful or hurtful after playing these games the children were given partners whom they could either support or oppose during the solving of a puzzle. The study showed that prosocial games increased helpful behavior and decreased hurtful behavior, whereas violent games made people more likely to be hurtful and less likely to be helpful. Earlier studies by the same researchers made a similar finding among college students, with prosocial games increasing empathy and willingness to cooperate and reducing feelings of hostility. Additionally, a 2009 study at Brigham Young University found that excessive video gaming had a negative effect on social behavior among college students, increasing the likelihood that a person would have poor relationships with friends and family and would engage in risky behaviors such as drinking and drug use.

person's emotion-related physiological reactions to whatever they are seeing. In one such study, it took only twenty minutes of playing games like *Duke Nukem* for test subjects to become less distressed at witnessing incidents of real-life violence.

However, not just violent video games but violent television shows and movies can cause this kind of desensitization, and some people say that all three are making violence more acceptable in society. But Nicholas Carnagey and Craig Anderson, who conducted an Iowa State study on desensitization related to video game playing, suspect that video games might be more effective than television and movies in desensitizing young people to violence because of the way the games package violence. They explain that violent video games for younger children, in particular, are "packaged in ways that are not too threatening, with cute cartoon-like characters, a total absence of blood and gore, and other features that make the overall experience a pleasant one. That arouses positive emotional reactions that are incongruent with normal negative reactions to violence. Older children consume increasingly threatening and realistic violence, but the increases are gradual and always in a way that is fun."[48]

Anderson is concerned about the way in which the video game industry eases kids into violence, providing them with more and more realistically violent games as they age. This approach, he suggests, make games "an effective systematic violence desensitization tool." But he believes that the issue is not just a matter of concern for scientists but for society as well. He says, "Whether modern societies want this to continue is largely a public policy question, not an exclusively scientific one."[49]

Benefits to Society

Anderson views desensitization as bad for society, and many others share this view because desensitization makes people more accepting of real-life violence and less likely to intervene to stop it. But video game experts argue that gaming also has benefits to society that might offset the harm of desensitization. For example, research has shown that playing video games, even violent ones, can reduce stress.

In fact, a recent study by Christopher J. Ferguson suggests that violent video games might even make people more upbeat. Ferguson reports, "It does seem that playing violent games may help reduce stress and make people less depressed and hostile."[50] While Ferguson admits that more studies are necessary to confirm this, he speculates that violent video games might help people vent their frustrations to the point where it might even be a good tool for therapists to use to help their patients work through negative emotions.

"It does seem that playing violent games may help reduce stress and make people less depressed and hostile."[50]

— Christopher Ferguson, associate professor of psychology and criminal justice at Texas A&M International University.

Video games can also teach people that failing can be an opportunity to learn. As James Paul Gee, author of *What Video Games Teach Us About Learning and Literacy*, notes, in school "failure is a big deal. Not so in games; just start over from the last save. A low cost for failure ensures that players will take risks, explore and try new things."[51] Part of this exploration also involves learning what other lifestyles are like. As gaming expert Frank Mainwaring notes,

Achievements in these games are attainable that are denied people in the real world. Who of us, given the materials and the time could become successful traders, traversing the globe, avoiding danger where necessary and fighting it off when not? These are the worlds that become unlocked, realms of imagination and fancy that are far more beneficial that sitting in front of a TV screen.[52]

Mainwaring also notes that critics are so focused on the violent elements of video games that they do not even see the games' positives aspects. "To many people 'beneficial' effects from games seem to be an oxymoron, that the two are mutually exclusive," he says. "Games are seen as a vast waste of time and energy that could be given over to other things. Games are often blamed for poor school performances and other outrageous behavior.[53]

Fans of *Bully*, for example, note that few critics of the game have noted that it shows bad actions having serious consequences. The Gamefaqs.com website reports:

The [school] staff also walks around, to make sure that everyone is keeping their noses clean. You can freely attack anyone you want, but depending on who you attack, [it] will result in a dire consequence. . . . Attacking a girl is an automatic detention on contact. The school has zero tolerance for female abuse. If you attack the staff, you will need to be ready to run away as quick as possible. If you are caught, you will have to serve detention. . . . You cannot beat up a grown woman or man in a city without the police chasing after you. This is much more serious than a school crime. If you are caught by the police, you will automatically be escorted back to school. There are many things that you can get punished for off and on school grounds.[54]

Consequently some gaming experts have lauded *Bully* for teaching kids that society considers certain actions to be bad enough to warrant serious consequences. But critics have pointed out that this contradicts the position such experts typically take in regard to first-person shooter games. That is, if *Bully* can teach kids that attacking girls, for example, is bad, then does a game like *Grand Theft Auto* not teach them that shooting people is good? Either video games have an influence on how people behave in real life or they do not—but research has yet to resolve this issue.

Encouraging Crime

Do video games encourage real-life bad behavior? A case out of Netherlands suggests the answer is yes—and no. In 2007 two Dutch teenagers forced a thirteen-year-old boy to log on to his account for the multiplayer online video game *RuneScape*. The pair then transferred two virtual items, an amulet and a mask, along with some virtual currency, to their own account. The objects were not real but because the pair had used violence and threats against their victim, police became involved and charged the perpetrators with theft. In 2008 both teens were found guilty and sentenced to perform community service, but one boy appealed his case to the Dutch Supreme Court. In January 2012 the Court upheld his conviction, dismissing his position that the game encouraged thievery. The Court said that although the point of the game was to take objects from other players, the boy's actions could not be blamed on the game.

Affecting Health and Well-Being

Consequently some people choose to concentrate instead on the physical side effects of game playing, which can affect society as well as individuals. For example, Constance Steinkuehler, senior policy analyst at the White House Office of Science and Technology Policy, has evaluated research into the effects of video gaming on society and concluded that its impact on human health and productivity is of more concern than whether such games inspire violent acts. In an April 2012 interview on her findings she said:

> The first research [into the impact of video games on society] really focused on its violent themes, for example, because, obviously, that's been sort of part of the American imagination of games as sort of leading to videogames violence, with issues like Columbine. And yet it turns out that many of those relationships just haven't borne out in the research, and new fields have emerged around looking at how games function as a means for turning screen time into activity time, thinking about: How can you use them to get up off the couch and get fit? How can you use them for improving problem-solving or scientific reasoning?[55]

Indeed, many people worry about what excessive gaming is doing to the human body in terms of fitness. Many studies have shown that excessive video game playing causes weight gain, not only because of the lack of activity that accompanies gaming but because gamers tend to have poor eating habits. In fact, a Canadian study published in 2011 in the *American Journal of Clinical Nutrition* showed that video gaming encourages mindless eating. Specifically, test subjects—who were teenage boys of normal weight—consumed an average of 163 more calories while gaming than they did while eating with no distractions, and many later said that while gaming they had been eating even when they were not hungry.

Excessive gaming can also cause aches and pains due to sitting in one place for long hours and using the hands over and over to control game play. Repetitive motion injuries to hands and arms can become severe enough to require surgery, and bad posture can cause chronic back and neck problems. In addition, people who

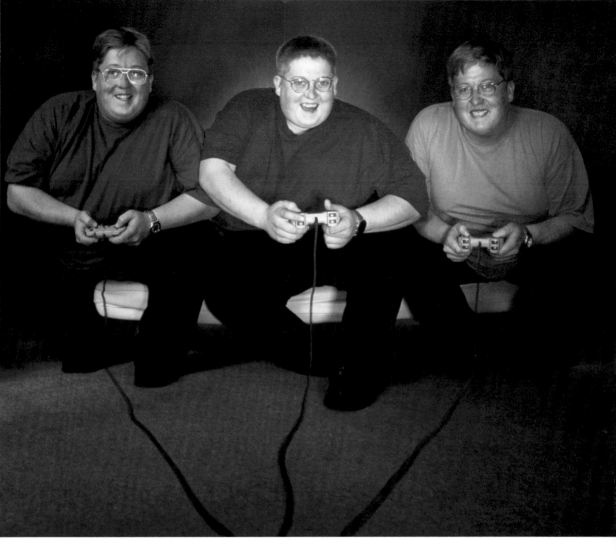

play video games for extended periods of time are more prone to experience migraine headaches because of the sustained concentration the activity requires and the strain that staring at the screen can put on the eyes. Many gamers also experience insomnia and other sleep disturbances due to overstimulation of the brain resulting from gaming prior to sleeping. All of these can lead to a drop in productivity or even an inability to work, the latter of which can cause social isolation.

Lack of physical activity and poor eating habits are common among those who spend hours playing video games. The result, some studies find, is weight gain.

Social Isolation?

Social isolation has long been an issue connected to video gaming. Parents often complain about the amount of time young people spend shut up in their rooms gaming, and when a school shooter is found to be a gamer the media typically begins searching for evidence that he was also a loner. Mainwaring, summing up the general public's attitude toward gamers, says, "To be a gamer is to be vilified by society: you are lazy because you aren't out in the sports fields playing sports; you are anti-social because you are in your room; pasty-faced, sociopathic and a murderer waiting to happen."[56]

But Mainwaring argues that while it might once have been correct that the majority of gamers were loners, today this is far from the case, especially given that gamers increasingly play with others over the Internet. He reports that video games "are increasingly social," with ones like *World of Warcraft* showing a "community gathering together regardless of race, colour or creed," and therefore: "The social interactivity we all need for healthy minds has been transposed from the physical to the virtual. Real life is increasingly hostile and isolated. . . . Games are reversing the isolationist trends of societies and governments across the globe, and forming their own groupings and networks."[57]

Mainwaring suggests that the online gaming community lacks the levels of discrimination found in the offline world, and research seems to bear this out. For example, in studying prejudices among online gamers, Joey J. Lee and Christopher M. Hoadley of Pennsylvania State University found that "the online environments provided a social space both to explore differences and to equalize them," thereby encouraging diversity. They explain:

> When meeting someone for the first time via face-to-face in real life, a person's physical appearance is typically judged first, which can often lead to prejudices or presuppositions based on assumptions of one's culture or visible attributes. In online environments . . . however, the reverse occurs; people get to know each other from the *inside out* . . . the content of one's character takes the forefront rather than biases or prejudices based on gender, race, age, sexuality, nationality, etc.[58]

Brooke Bliven and Marin Abernethy, both experts on gaming and social change, note that the work of Lee and Hoadley, among others, has shown that gamers "can take what they have attained from role-playing games and apply it to their real-world social interactions." They add:

> Traditional games [e.g. board games and cards] as well as video games [in arcades] have been bringing people together for years and it was never until recently that the image of gamers changed from being a typical activity to one that is frowned upon by so many people. These assumptions are made without proper knowledge of what these gamers and their culture are about. Games can create a place where one can feel comfortable, where discrimination is limited. A shy introvert can become a fearless leader, friendships can form without judgments of the physical intervening, and tools for accepting differences can be brought into the real world.[59]

But critics argue that a lack of discrimination among online gamers does not make up for the apparent racism and sexism displayed in the games these people play. They point to games like *Ethnic Cleansing* (2002), which allows players to take on the role of an anti-Semite to kill not only Jews but blacks and Latinos, as evidence that at least some violent video games have no redeeming features whatsoever. Moreover, some critics argue that such games are so damaging to society that their production should not be allowed—a position that gamers counter in part by pointing out that critics sometimes condemn games without even knowing their content.

"Games can create a place where one can feel comfortable, where discrimination is limited."[59]

— Brooke Bliven and Marin Abernethy, experts on gaming and social change.

Facts

- In 2005, as part of an effort to make it a crime in the United States to sell games rated "Mature" or "Adults Only" to minors, then-senator of New York Hillary Clinton specifically cited desensitization as the reason such a law was needed.

- Surveys conducted in 2012 indicate that among teens aged twelve to seventeen, most think that violence has increased in their schools.

- One in five young people admit to having engaged in bullying on at least one occasion.

- According to a 2011 report by the Pew Internet and American Life Project, 55 percent of young people who encounter one person bullying another online decide not to go to the victim's aid.

- According to a study at the University of Pittsburgh as reported in the *American Journal of Preventative Medicine* in June 2012, when video games were employed to help people work through psychological problems, the outcome of psychological therapy was improved by 69 percent.

- In May 2012 Professor Richard Davidson of the University of Wisconsin–Madison received a $1.39 million grant from the Bill & Melinda Gates Foundation to develop and test two video games intended to help eighth graders develop and/or strengthen empathy.

- A Michigan State University study reported in November 2011 found that playing video games increases a young person's creativity as expressed through drawings and stories, regardless of whether the games played are violent or nonviolent.

Do Violent Video Games Encourage Addictive Behavior?

In February 2011 spectators in a Philadelphia, Pennsylvania, courtroom were stunned to hear the circumstances surrounding a murder committed on Thanksgiving evening the previous year. In court, sixteen-year-old Kendall Anderson confessed that he had bludgeoned his sleeping mother over twenty times with a claw hammer, and upon realizing she might still be alive he tried to incinerate her in his kitchen's oven. When he decided this was impossible, he beat her in the head with a chair leg, and once he was sure she was dead he dragged her body into the alley behind his house, hid it with debris, and called police to report his mother missing. Her body was not found until two days later.

But perhaps even more shocking than what Anderson did was why he did it: He was upset that his mother had forbidden him to play video games as punishment for having stolen a laptop, and after about ninety minutes of arguing with her about this, she took his PlayStation away. For three hours afterward Anderson paced back and forth in his room, agitated, trying to figure out how to get the gaming device back, and finally he decided to kill his mother. Later he said he regretted this decision because she was the only person in his life who cared about him.

Media Response

When the details of this story became known, many in the media called the case an example of video game addiction, whereby players become so obsessed with playing games that they get upset, anxious, and agitated when their access to these games is cut off. The notion that Anderson was addicted to his games explains why some reporters spoke of the young man as suffering from withdrawal during the three hours he was deciding what to do about his lost PlayStation. People who are addicted to certain drugs have similar symptoms when they stop using the drugs, and the term "withdrawal" refers to the state of experiencing these symptoms. However, Anderson himself did not blame a video game addiction. Instead he said he simply could not stand fighting with his mother anymore.

Still, media preoccupation with video game addiction in association with the crime persisted, even as some reporters stepped forward to argue that there is no such thing. For example, *Huffington Post* reporter Kirsten West Savali said, "We can speculate that Anderson was in the throes of this addiction when he murdered his mother. . . . However, there's another equally plausible reason: He's just another spoiled juvenile delinquent who didn't consider the long-reaching ramifications of his barbaric actions."[60]

Savali further argues that as the son of a single mother, many other factors in Kendall Anderson's life could probably have influenced him negatively aside from video gaming. She says:

> Where was Kendall's father? Why was Kendall being accused of theft? Were there issues inside the home? Were they struggling financially? While there are too many unresolved questions to play this child's judge and jury, I do know you can only get out of a child what is put in to them. In this young man's case, violence, selfishness and

rage seemed to embolden him to kill. His actions were unconscionable, and inexcusable, and hopefully he receives the lesson in accountability he needs while behind bars.[61]

This suggests that society is providing Anderson with an excuse for his behavior—and as Jason Krell, a columnist with the University of Arizona's *Daily Wildcat* newspaper, notes, the possible excuses in such cases are usually ample. He says, "Yes, the PlayStation triggered this act of violence, but I doubt the only reason [Anderson] committed this heinous crime was because he couldn't stand the idea of not being able to play it. There are nonviolent cases, too, that might support the existence of video game addiction, but there are always other underlying problems."[62]

A gamer himself, Krell equates excessive gaming with any other engrossing activity, such as reading a book you cannot put down, and he argues that engaging in such an activity is always a matter of choice. He says:

> "I just wanted to play video games more than any of those other things."[63]
>
> — Jason Krell, gamer.

> Yes, some people take video games to a whole other level. I myself spent far too much time playing "World of Warcraft" in high school and skipped out on spending time with friends and didn't do homework that I probably should have. Would I call that an addiction though? Absolutely not. Instead of blaming these arguably poor life choices on an "addiction," I took responsibility and said the truth—I just wanted to play video games more than any of those other things.[63]

Addictive Features

Some psychiatrists, though, do believe that video game addiction is a real condition. In fact, in 2007 the American Medical Association stated that there might be as many as 5 million game addicts aged eight to eighteen in the United States. More recently, in 2011 Douglas A. Gentile of the Iowa State University Media Research Lab announced the results of a two-year study that found that as many as one in ten school-age children in the United States could be video game addicts. Based on these and other studies, experts

An extreme gamer who regularly rents space at an Internet café in China has fallen asleep at his computer. Avid gamers say the appeal of playing a game for hours is not unlike reading an engrossing book all night long but others say excessive gaming is a sign of addiction.

in mental disorders have debated adding video game addiction to *The Diagnostic and Statistical Manual of Mental Disorders* (DSM) as a recognized mental disorder. (Published by the American Psychiatric Association, the DSM is an official guide to known mental disorders, including addictions.)

Video game addiction has not been included in this guide thus far, though, because scientists have yet to determine conclusively whether the brains of people suffering from what appears to be video game addiction show physical effects similar to those with known addictive substances. In cases of drug addiction, for example, the use of certain drugs can increase the amount of a chemical called dopamine in the brain, which then responds to this artificially induced increase by reducing the amount of dopamine it produces naturally. This means that the brain is now dependent on drugs for its normal level of dopamine—a chemical involved in such things as motivation, mood, memory, attention, and voluntary movement. As a result, without the drugs the person feels bad, and with the drugs the person feels good. The bad period is the withdrawal period.

Physical Evidence

Without evidence that the brain actually changes in this way because of video gaming, psychiatrists are unwilling to commit to the notion that video game "addictions" can actually cause withdrawal. Some researchers, however, believe that enough physical evidence exists to prove that video game playing can trigger physical responses that make it an actual addiction, something that makes you feel good when done and bad when stopped. For example, Dave Grossman says that the violent component in video games can affect people in much the same way as a known addictive substance can, reporting that children in particular "are riveted by violent television, movies and video games. Their heartbeat goes up, their respiration goes up. . . . [Violence] is the addicting ingredient, as nicotine is the addictive ingredient in tobacco."[64]

New studies suggest that video gaming causes some changes in the brain as well. For example, a November 2011 study involving young men who played violent first-person shooter video games for ten hours a week showed, based on magnetic resonance imaging (MRI) of the brain, that gaming reduced activity in areas of the brain responsible for inhibition, attention, and controlling emotion. The effects were not permanent; once the gaming stopped, the brain began to revert to its normal state. Nonetheless, the changes were significant enough to warrant further study.

In January 2012 Chinese researchers announced the results of another study in which the brain scans of nongamers aged fourteen to twenty-one were compared with those of gamers in the same age group who had been diagnosed with Internet Addiction Disorder (IAD), a recognized disorder in China. The brain scans of the gamers had patterns of abnormal white matter that were absent in nongamers' scans. These patterns appeared in a part of the brain containing nerve fibers that transmit signals to other parts of the brain involved in decision making, impulse control, and emotions.

David Walsh, a child psychologist who has studied the relationship between violent video games and physical aggression, says that

Death by Addiction

On July 13, 2012, an eighteen-year-old known only as Chuang walked into an Internet café in Tainan, Taiwan, at around noon and began playing the online video game *Diablo 3* in a private room. He stayed there for two days straight without eating or drinking until he collapsed and later died at a local hospital. A few months earlier, another man in New Taipei, Taiwan, died slumped in a chair, his hands still on the keyboard, after playing video games for twenty-three hours straight. In 2005 a similar death occurred in South Korea after twenty-eight-year-old Seungseob Lee played *Starcraft* at an Internet café for fifty hours straight. Physicians later determined that all three young men had died of a heart attack due to sitting so long in one position. Scientists have found that this can cause blood clots in the legs which can then migrate to the heart to cause sudden cardiac arrest.

the brains of young people are particularly vulnerable to such effects. The reason, he says, lies in the way that the brain develops. He explains, "The teenage brain is different from the adult brain. The impulse control center of the brain, the part of the brain that enables us to think ahead, consider consequences, manage urges . . . that's under construction during the teenage years. In fact, the wiring of that is not completed until the early 20s."[65] Walsh also says that if a person comes from a troubled background, the impulse control center can be even more compromised after prolonged gaming. Therefore some see this as the reason young people like Kendall Anderson sometimes lash out when denied their video games.

Mindless Escapism

In addition, problems with impulse control can lead people to reach for known addictive substances such as alcohol when they know they should not. This might explain why gamers exhibit behaviors that others see as signs of an addiction. As examples of such behaviors involving players of *World of Warcraft* (WoW), journalist Rhodri Marsden, who tried WoW herself to study its effects, reports, "For those who have 'addictive personalities,' playing WoW is not so benign an activity. There are plenty of stories of gaming leading to relationship breakdowns."[66] As an example Marsden cites the case of Wendy Kays, who watched her marriage fall apart after her husband became addicted to online gaming, which she likened to a drug addiction.

For gamer Jon Appleyard, playing WoW three nights a week is akin to having alcoholic drinks after work as a way to relax and unwind. He says, "I'll admit I use it as a comfort thing, a dependable way of escaping from everyday life. If I wasn't playing WoW, I'd probably be getting wasted down the pub."[67] Others have lauded gaming for its mindlessness. For example, Nina Simon, an expert in participatory learning, says, "There are a variety of social pressures that encourage us to keep moving, to read a new book, to try a new trick, to go to a new film, rather than doing the same old thing. Not so with addictive games. Addictive games allow us to wallow in skills we already have, to set our brains aside awhile and just do."[68]

Lost Work

However, gaming can easily get out of hand, causing people to lose sleep, skip work, and otherwise shirk responsibilities when they cannot control their impulse to play games. One of the most well-publicized examples of this involves Quinn Pitcock, a former All-American defensive tackle for the Indianapolis Colts NFL football team. He became so addicted to playing *Call of Duty* on his Xbox 360 that he stopped playing football. "I couldn't put [the game controller] down," he says.[69]

In fact, his addiction was so bad that even when he took measures to prevent himself from having access to the game, he sought out ways to play. "I broke about four games in half," he reports, "burned them, microwaved them, put a torch to them, letting my aggression out to get rid of them. But the next day, I was at Target buying another game." Eventually he was diagnosed with depression and attention deficit hyperactivity disorder (ADHD) in addition to video game addiction, but he believes that his problem ultimately lies in "a brain that doesn't quite work the way everybody else's brain does."[70]

Since video gaming is not widely recognized as an addiction in the United States, Americans who cannot control their impulse to play such games often have trouble finding people sympathetic to their plight and cannot figure out how to help themselves. Psychologist Ryan G. Van Cleave, summing up the typical situation for a video game junkie, says, "He's hooked. Even though he admits he's tired of the games and wishes he could quit, he doesn't, and not understanding how that contradiction can exist makes him feel small, disempowered, and afraid. From there comes the inevitable shame and guilt spiral into utter despair, which he more than likely is doomed to endure alone."[71]

Addiction Treatment Centers

Someone who is addicted to drugs or alcohol has the option of living at an addiction treatment center, a place that helps people go through "detox," or detoxification, to rid his or her body of its dependence on these toxic physical substances. In some places, game addicts can find centers that help them through a form of detox. The first residential treatment program for gaming addiction was started in 2006 in the city of Amsterdam in Netherlands. Known as the Smith & Jones Addiction Consultants, its treatment program involves therapy to understand the reasons for the addiction and lessons in how to avoid gaming in a world where computers are seemingly everywhere. Center director Keith Bakker says that in this way a gaming addiction is like an eating addiction, because whereas alcoholics and drug addicts can stay away from places where those addictive substances are sold, food and computers are a regular part of daily life.

Common Characteristics

In order to prevent these problems, some studies have sought to identify the common characteristics of people prone to developing gaming obsessions. This was the aim of a two-year study led by Gentile, the results of which were released in the journal *Pediatrics* in January 2011. The study examined elementary and middle school students in Singapore over a two-year period to identify risk factors and personal attributes that might lead a child to become what it called an obsessive or pathological gamer. The research found that such gamers tended to be more impulsive and less empathetic than other children and had more difficulty keeping their emotions in control. They were also more likely to be socially incompetent.

The study also found that once a gaming obsession was in full force, the affected gamers were typically depressed and anxious and exhibited social phobias. They were also more likely to be bullied, and many engaged in acts of aggression themselves and/or had fantasies of doing so. The study also found that the children who developed gaming obsessions were still obsessed by the end of the two-year study, suggesting that their problem would continue unabated unless someone or something intervened to make or encourage them to abandon their obsession.

Encouraging Addiction

Obsessive gamers do not easily abandon their obsession, however, because the gaming industry does so much to encourage an addiction to video games. Specifically, game designers add features to their games that are designed to get people hooked on playing them, using aspects of behavioral science developed by B.F. Skinner beginning in the 1940s. An American psychologist, Skinner discovered that behavior could be controlled by rewarding desired actions in certain ways and at certain times, thereby conditioning animals or people to continue acting in those ways.

For example, Skinner found that he could train rats to press a lever by rewarding them with food pellets. However, he discovered that if he provided a pellet every time the rat pushed the lever, the

Detroit Lions defensive lineman Quinn Pitcock (95) is flagged for a low hit during a 2011 preseason game against the Cleveland Browns. Pitcock, who is no longer with the Lions, had earlier played for the Indianapolis Colts but left the team because of an addiction to playing the video game Call of Duty.

rat would often wait to press it because he knew that food would always arrive when he did. On the other hand, if Skinner rewarded the lever-pushing at random intervals, the rat would push the lever over and over again, with shorter and shorter intervals in between presses, obsessed with finding out when the next pellet would arrive. This is similar to the behavior of gamblers playing a slot machine that only rewards them with money payouts at random intervals.

In video games the rewards might include new skills and abilities, acquired game objects like weapons, and points that eventually allow the player to move up a level in the game. All of these are incentives for people to keep playing; indeed, research has shown that players invest more time in a game just as they are about to level up. Gamers also become more obsessed with play when a game threatens to take an earned item away if it is not used by a certain point.

Game designer Erin Hoffman says that simplicity is another aspect of what she calls "addictive game mechanics." Games with clear problems and clear solutions tend to be more addictive, along with those in which most actions produce consequences with "an element of randomness, unpredictability, and intermittent reward" so that gamers do not always know what is going to happen. She adds that when games are simple and clear, they work the brain "without requiring the engagement of messier things like grey area judgment, ethics, social repercussion, or any of the myriad other complex elements we have to deal with in the reality of our daily lives. The reward system and its . . . consequences ensure that we achieve a variable but deeply satisfying result from our simple, clear action."[72]

In an article called "5 Creepy Ways Video Games Are Trying to Get You Addicted," writer and editor David Wong agrees that video games rely on intermittent rewards to hook players. But he also points out that these measurable rewards provide a type of accomplishment that most people do not get elsewhere. "This is what most of us don't get in everyday life—quick, tangible rewards," he says. "How much harder would we work at the office if we got this, and could measure our progress toward it?"[73] Indeed, video game accomplishments are typically easy to measure and track, and they are judged objectively rather than subjectively. For example, to judge a person's success as a first-person shooter, all one would have to do is check his or her number of kills.

> "This is what most of us don't get in everyday life—quick, tangible rewards."[73]
>
> — Writer and editor David Wong, on achievements within a video game.

Those Other Activities

Wong believes that video games have become "incredibly efficient at delivering the sense of accomplishment that people used to get from their education or career" and says that video game addiction is a growing problem "because the real world's system of rewards is so much more slow and cruel than we expected it to be [when we were kids]."[74] But Hoffman suggests that instead of looking at the addiction problem in terms of what might be missing from the gamer's life, people should consider what the gamer might be avoiding. She explains:

Addiction is not about what you DO, but what you DON'T DO because of the replacement of the addictive behavior. The reason why what defines addiction for one person may not define addiction for another person . . . is because addiction is not about the action, but about the individual person. This is why merely resisting addiction of any kind is not enough. This is why—although some activities are more broadly compelling than others—virtually any activity can become an addiction. What addictive behavior does is reveal underlying anxiety (and often depression, which itself is nebulous) and lack of desire to perform the things we're "supposed to" be doing.[75]

But when people do not do what they are supposed to do, society can suffer. Important jobs might be left undone, resources might be strained. To prevent this possibility, society often criticizes people who devote too many hours to a game, sport, or hobby, admonishing them not to waste time like that. But as Marsden points out, such judgments hinge on values that not everyone shares. She says, "In two weeks as a subscriber to WoW, I played it for some 27 hours—a shocking statistic. How could that time have been better spent? That leads to questions surrounding the point of our existence: is learning to knit or going to the cinema any more use than emerging triumphant from Ragefire Chasm having vanquished Jergosh the Invoker?"[76]

Kays responds to Marsden by saying, "That's the question gamers need to address. If people have thought about this, and decide to choose gaming, that's fine—they should go ahead and have a great time. But the ones who haven't—and particularly if they have responsibility for children—just need to be asked the question, otherwise in five years they'll wonder where all that time went."[77]

Facts

- According to a study reported in 2009 in the *International Journal of Mental Health and Addiction*, 41 percent of online video gamers say they do it to escape from the real world.

- Studies have shown that males are more prone to video game addiction than females.

- Research conducted in 2010 indicates that multiplayer online role-playing games are the most likely to trigger addictive behavior.

- In 2011 Rebecca Colleen Christie of Las Cruces, New Mexico, was convicted of murder after her addiction to playing *World of Warcraft* resulted in her three-year-old daughter dying of malnutrition and dehydration.

- In June 2012 a fourteen-year-old boy in India strangled a sixty-nine-year-old neighbor in order to steal her jewelry so he could afford a PlayStation game player.

Should the Sale of Violent Video Games Be Restricted?

In June 2011 the US Supreme Court issued a ruling that angered people opposed to violent video games. The high court sided with a lower court ruling that a California law making it illegal to rent or sell such games to minors is unconstitutional. The games at issue included images of people being killed, maimed, dismembered, or sexually assaulted, and when then-governor of California Arnold Schwarzenegger signed the legislation into law in 2005, he said, "Today I signed legislation to ensure parent involvement in determining which video games are appropriate for their children. The bill I signed will require violent video games to be clearly labeled and not sold to children under 18 years old. Many of these games are made for adults, and choosing games that are appropriate for kids should be a decision made by their parents."[78]

After the Supreme Court ruling against the law, the gaming industry also cited parental involvement as an important factor in game purchases by youth. Patricia Vance of the Entertainment Software Rating Board (ESRB) said, "In striking this law the Court has made clear that the video game industry effectively empowers parents to be the ones to decide which games are right for their children."[79] Schwarzenegger was focusing on the fact that the law would keep children from buying violent video games without their parents' knowledge, while Vance was suggesting that parents alone should have the right to decide whether their children can buy such a game. Supreme Court justice Antonin Scalia, writing the majority opinion for the court, agrees with Vance. He writes, "No doubt a state possesses legitimate power to protect children from harm. But that does not include a free-floating power to restrict the ideas to which children may be exposed."[80]

First Amendment Rights

In making its decision the Supreme Court was not addressing parental rights but First Amendment rights. Ratified in 1791 as part of the Bill of Rights, the First Amendment guarantees the right of free speech, which means that people must be free to express themselves without government interference. This right applies not only to verbal expression but to written and visual expression as well. Consequently the Supreme Court struck down the California law on the grounds that it violated the First Amendment. In the court's opinion of the law, Scalia writes, "Video games qualify for First Amendment protection. Like protected books, plays and movies, they communicate ideas through familiar literary devices and features distinctive to the medium."[81]

Prior to this ruling, the court had not specifically provided First Amendment protection to video games. However, decades earlier it had addressed the subject in regard to books and movies and more recently in connection with videos of animal cruelty. Shortly before the 2011 video game decision, the court struck down a federal law that made it a crime to sell videos depicting cruelty to animals. The court reasoned that it should not create a new category of speech that rested outside the protections of the First Amendment. Justice Sonia Sotomayor referenced this case while evaluating the video game case, questioning how the court could say that one category of speech, video games, should be set apart from others and given fewer protections than the rest.

Scalia brought up this same issue to attorneys arguing the video game case. "What's a deviant violent video game?" he asked them. "As opposed to what? A normal violent video game?" He also expressed concern that such judgments might eventually be applied to books as well, saying, "Some of the Grimm's fairy tales are quite grim. Are you going to ban them too?"[82]

But Justice Stephen G. Breyer countered that common sense dictates that the government should be able to prevent young people from having access to certain images, such as the violent and painful torture of women and children that most members of a civilized society can agree are repugnant. And indeed, the Supreme Court has already limited children's access to one category of speech: the sexually explicit. In 1968 the court upheld the government's right to regulate the distribution of sexual materials to minors, and in 1973 it declared that obscenity was not protected by the First Amendment.

The Miller Test

As part of this 1973 decision, known as *Miller v. California*, the court established a test that could be used to determine whether a form of speech or expression should be deemed obscene. Known as the Miller test, this evaluation has three components, all of which need to be satisfied in order for the work to be considered obscene and therefore not protected under the First Amendment. First, the average—not the most sensitive—person in a community must, according to the standards of that community, find that the work elicits prurient (lustful) interest; second, the work must show or describe sexual activity in a way that is clearly and obviously offensive; and third, the work must have absolutely no literary, artistic, political, or scientific value as determined by what is reasonable to Americans as a whole (as opposed to simply members of a single community). Using this test, courts have consistently found that child pornography, for example, is not protected under the First Amendment.

Opponents of violent video games were hoping that the Supreme Court, in deciding the 2011 California case, would come up with a similar test that would separate violent video games from more benign offerings, thereby allowing states to deem cer-

"Some of the Grimm's fairy tales are quite grim. Are you going to ban them too?"[82]

— US Supreme Court justice Antonin Scalia.

In 2005 California governor Arnold Schwarzenegger signs into law a bill restricting the sale and rental of violent video games to minors. The US Supreme Court later overturned the law, saying it violated First Amendment protections.

tain games inappropriate for children. Indeed, Breyer indirectly linked video games to the Miller test by suggesting that if children could be prevented from accessing pornography they could also be prevented from accessing violent games. In a dissent to the court's finding he writes:

> What sense does it make to forbid selling to a 13-year-old boy a magazine with an image of a nude woman while protecting a sale to that 13-year-old of an interactive video game in which he actively, but virtually, binds and gags the woman, then tortures and kills her? What kind of First Amendment would permit the government to protect

children by restricting sales of that extremely violent video game only when the woman—bound, gagged, tortured, and killed—is also topless?[83]

Other Violent Media

Attorneys also presented the court with studies suggesting that violent video games harm children by making players more violent. The justices dismissed these studies as flawed and added that accepting their premise would mean other forms of media violence would have to be restricted as well. The court explains:

> Psychological studies purporting to show a connection between exposure to violent video games and harmful effects on children do not prove that such exposure causes minors to act aggressively. Any demonstrated effects are both small and indistinguishable from effects produced by other media. Since California has declined to restrict those other media, e.g., Saturday morning cartoons, its video-game regulation is wildly underinclusive, raising serious doubts about whether the State is pursuing the interest it invokes or is instead disfavoring a particular speaker or viewpoint.[84]

The justices also rejected arguments that suggested violent video games had no literary or artistic value, an aspect of creative work deemed important by the Miller test. The court responded to this point by noting that video games communicate ideas and messages using characters, dialogue, and other literary devices similar to those in books and movies. Moreover, Scalia adds that while reading great literature is "unquestionably more cultured and intellectually edifying than playing Mortal Kombat, . . . crudely violent video games, tawdry TV shows, and cheap novels and magazines are no less forms of speech"[85] than great literature and are therefore just as deserving of First Amendment protection.

At least two of the justices, however, were concerned about the notion that striking down the ban meant merchants could sell violent games directly to children without parents being involved. In expressing this view, Breyer argues that sometimes "choices are made for children—by their parents, by their teachers, and by the people acting democratically through their governments,"[86] without this necessarily being an abridgement of a child's rights. And Justice Clarence Thomas argues that because of minors' dependency on their parents, "'the freedom of speech,' as originally understood, does not include a right to speak to minors [or a right of minors to access speech] without going through the minors' parents or guardians."[87] Nonetheless, the court decision means that government cannot directly shield children from violent expression.

European Ratings

In July 2012, the United Kingdom abandoned its own video game rating system in favor of a system already used by thirty other European countries. Known as PEGI, or Pan European Game Information, and developed by the Interactive Software Federation of Europe (ISFE), this rating system has been in use since April 2003. Like the US ratings system, it is designed to help parents make decisions about video game purchases for their children. PEGI has five categories: 3, 7, 12, 16, and 18, with each number representing the youngest age for which a game is suitable. Ratings are also accompanied by descriptions of content much like those in the United States. For example, a rating of 18 (for age 18 and up) means the game may contain, among other things, graphic violence, vulgar language, strong sexual content, gambling, the glamorization of drug use, and/or discrimination. The one major difference between the European and US ratings systems is that US ratings are overseen by game manufacturers. The European ratings are set by an independent group and overseen by various professionals that include child psychologists, academics, and legal experts involved in child protection.

Game Ratings

In other countries, however, governments do ban certain violent video games. For example, Australia currently does not allow *Mortal Kombat, Postal, Postal 2,* and several other video games to be sold due to their violent content. Brazil has also banned several violent games, including *Bully, Doom, Duke Nukem 3D, Mortal Kombat, Postal, and Grand Theft Auto.* In China, many games have been banned not only because of violence but because they show sex, drug use, or certain criminal acts or because they defame the Chinese government in some way. Russia, on the other hand, does not ban any games, nor do they have a formal ratings board to guide parents in deciding which games are appropriate for children.

The ratings board in the United States was established in 1994, when the gaming industry began to worry that the government would step in to censor game content. Game ratings were modeled after the ratings system established by the motion picture industry in the 1960s, whereby parents are informed about the appropriateness of a film for a certain age category. Video game ratings offer the same kind of guidance; ratings include EC (Early Childhood), E (Everyone), E-10+ (Everyone age ten and older), T (Teen, meaning age thirteen and older), M (Mature, meaning players seventeen and older), and AO (Adults Only). Game developers also generally put comments on the packaging of a game indicating what elements of the game prompted a particular rating. These might include "blood and gore," "intense violence," or "strong sexual content."

Prior to the Supreme Court ruling on California's ban, merchants would point out this information to parents concerned about the games their children are buying. Now, though, confusion over the ruling has made some merchants, especially in California, hesitant to mention age guidelines at all. This results in more parents making purchases without being aware of a game's content. In addition, young people are increasingly buying their own games, either in a retail store or via the Internet, without their parents being involved in the transaction. This is perhaps one reason that in a recent survey, 50 percent of teenage boys under the age of seventeen admitted to having played games rated Mature.

Some parents also knowingly buy their under-seventeen children a game rated Mature. This might be because they do not understand exactly what is meant by terms like "blood and gore." That is, they do not realize just how bloody a game is, for example, or just how extreme certain acts of "intense violence" might be.

However, studies in the UK, which has a ratings system for video games similar to the one in the United States, indicate that parents who ignore warnings related to violence in a game typically do so because they believe game violence will not harm their child.

The Family Entertainment and Protection Act

Antigaming activists have long been concerned about the fact that the video game industry is responsible for determining the ratings for its own games. These activists believe that financial concerns give the industry an incentive to misrepresent the degree and/or type of violence in a game in order to spare it a harsh rating. Industry leaders insist that they do not do this, and there is no evidence that they have. Nonetheless, federal legislators attempted to address such concerns in 2005 by creating a bill called the Family Entertainment Protection Act, whereby the Federal Trade Commission rather than the gaming industry's Entertainment Software Rating Board would oversee the rating system and determine game ratings. However, the bill also included penalties for store owners who sold games rated Mature or Adults Only to minors, and when courts began finding such penalties unconstitutional, backers of the Family Entertainment Protection Act decided not to bring the bill up for a vote before Congress.

The Entertainment Software Rating Board has created a ratings system for video games. Ratings such as M for mature and E for everyone (visible in the lower left-hand corner of each game) appear on all video games sold in the United States.

Researcher Jurgen Freund says, "Most parents think their child is mature enough so that these games will not influence them." Freund also reports that parents are generally far more concerned about how many hours their children spend playing video games than about exactly which games they are playing. While parents might not like the content of a particular game, he says, "they did not prohibit the game." Freund's research has also revealed that most parents know little about current video games, are un-interested in them, and therefore do not care to research the latest games to find out what kind of content might be in the games their children are asking to play. Consequently, he says, "parents are too divorced from what teenagers play."[88]

Societal Pressures

Despite such studies, the gaming industry insists that ratings sys-tems—combined with informed, involved parenting—are the best way to ensure that children do not have access to violent games. But advocates of gaming restrictions say there is a better way to ensure that children do not have access to violent games: Create a cultural climate in which it is considered extremely wrong for children to play such games. In fact, some of these advocates say that society needs to adopt the philosophy that violent games are bad for everybody. For example, Dave Grossman says:

> Today we have the moral courage to tell someone, "Don't you dare get in that car in this drunken state. I am going to call you a taxi." We have achieved a moral outrage about drunken drivers, and drunks are now modifying their behaviour because of this moral outrage. Similarly we now say, "I'd rather you didn't light up a cigarette, please. This is a non-smoking area." When we have the moral courage to get up and say so, then we have achieved a moral indignation that truly modifies a smoker's behaviour. In the same way, we need to say to kids about violent games, "That's sick."[89]

Indeed, when a particularly repugnant game is released, public pressure does have an effect on how that game is received. Sometimes it even results in a game being voluntarily banned by a store or group of stores. For example, in 2009 American retailers agreed to stop selling a Japanese-produced video game titled *RapeLay* that enables players to commit sexual violence against a female victim. Leigh Alexander, news editor of an online video game review site, found the game so offensive that she said, "The interactive assaults are difficult to endure if you have a conscience."[90]

"The interactive assaults are difficult to endure if you have a conscience."[90]

— Leigh Alexander in reviewing *RapeLay*, a game featuring sexual assaults.

Antigaming Lawsuits

Absent public pressure, some antigaming activists have sought to hinder the sale of violent video games by launching lawsuits to stop their release. Former attorney Jack Thompson is the best-known proponent of this tactic. He has also sued on behalf of people who have lost family members to violence that Thompson believes was ultimately the result of playing violent video games.

But Paul Smith, an attorney who specializes in First Amendment issues and has represented video game companies in court, says, "If you start saying that we're going to sue people because one individual out there read their book or played their game and decided to become a criminal, there is no stopping point. It's a huge new swath of censorship that will be imposed on the media."[91]

Antigaming lawsuits also impose economic hardships on game developers and marketers. For the most part, however, the industry is extremely profitable, bringing in billions of dollars a year. And as Kenneth Turan, film critic with the *Los Angeles Times*, says, "Violence sells and, as numerous observers have commented, it is so ingrained in Western civilization that even a core document like the Bible is rife with it."[92]

In fact, not only does violence sell, but in terms of video games it sells disproportionally more than nonviolence. In 2010, for example, games rated M and therefore intended only for players age seventeen and older made up just 5 percent of available games, yet five of the ten top-selling games of the year (selling in the millions) were rated M: *Call of Duty: Black Ops, Halo: Reach, Red Dead Redemption, Call of Duty: Modern Warfare 2,* and *Assassin's Creed: Brotherhood.* Given such profits, the gaming industry is understandably unwilling to stop producing violent video games.

Making Games That Sell

It was not always this way, though. In the 1980s prominent video game companies Atari and Nintendo declared that they would never feature graphic violence in their games. According to Nolan Bushnell, one of the founders of Atari, "We had an internal rule that we wouldn't allow violence against people. You could blow up a tank or you could blow up a flying saucer, but you couldn't blow up people. We felt that was not good form, and we adhered to that all during my tenure."[93] Nintendo had a similar rule, but it hurt the company after other game developers began making violent games like *Death Race.* As George Harrison, vice president

"We had an internal rule that we wouldn't allow violence against people. You could blow up a tank or you could blow up a flying saucer, but you couldn't blow up people."[93]

— Nolan Bushnell, a founder of Atari, on the company's early years.

of marketing for Nintendo during this period, reports, "We got a lot of plaudits for [the code of ethics] in public—and got killed in the sales arena."[94]

As a result, sales concerns won out over ethical concerns, and the industry as a whole became mindful of the importance of maintaining its right to continue producing violent video games. At the same time, game developers gradually realized that violence alone does not sell games; the features of the game have to be good, too. In fact, the game usually has to be excellent in order to withstand the controversies and public condemnation likely to arise upon its release. Consequently game companies put a lot of time and money into developing their violent video games, and the result is usually praise from gamers. As gaming expert Evan Narcisse says, "No one goes into the game store thinking 'I'm going to buy an M-rated game today!' Just as in movies and books and music, people make purchasing decisions based on content and quality. It's no coincidence that all those M-rated games in the top ten happened to be very good."[95]

By "good," Narcisse does not mean good for society, but good in terms of enjoyable gameplay. Antigaming activists say this kind of focus on individual enjoyment rather than the greater good of society is part of the problem because it makes people forget that violent games might impact players in ways not yet known. And as Turan notes, "If we do have to have violence in popular culture, we have to stop pretending there are no consequences to having it be so easily available."[96] What these consequences might be, however, remains a matter of controversy.

> "If we do have to have violence in popular culture, we have to stop pretending there are no consequences to having it be so easily available."[96]
>
> — Kenneth Turan, film critic with the *Los Angeles Times*.

Facts

- More than 46 million American households now have at least one video game system.

- In 2010 the gaming industry brought in $66 billion worldwide.

- Gaming industry experts believe that online sales of games will soon surpass retail sales of games.

- According to game designer and industry expert Jane McGonigal, gamers spend 3 billion hours a week playing online video games.

- During the period from 1995 to 2008, when the number and sales of violent video games jumped dramatically, the arrest rate for juvenile murders fell 71.9 percent, and the arrest rate for all juvenile violent crimes declined 49.3 percent.

- According to game maker Activision, between November 2010 and January 2011, 62 billion virtual people died in *Call of Duty: Black Ops*.

Source Notes

Introduction: An Obsession with Violence

1. Paul Tassi, "The Idiocy of Blaming Video Games for the Norway Massacre," *Forbes*, April 19, 2012. www.forbes.com.

2. Quoted in Rebecca Leung, "Can a Video Game Lead to Murder?," *60 Minutes*, CBS News, February 9, 2005. www.cbsnews.com.

3. Quoted in Daniel J. DeNoon, "Do Video Games Really Spark Bad Behavior?," Fox News, August 19, 2005. www.foxnews.com.

4. Quoted in Scott Steinberg, "The Benefits of Video Games," ABC News, December 26, 2011. http://abcnews.go.com.

Chapter One: What Are the Origins of the Violent Video Game Controversy?

5. Quoted in Mark J.P. Wolf, ed., *The Medium of the Video Game*. Austin: University of Texas Press, 2001, p. 40.

6. Quoted in Benjamin H. Alexander, "Impact of Computers on Human Behavior," *Vital Speeches of the Day*, January 1, 1983, p. 186.

7. Ben Kuchera, "*Duke Nukem Forever*: Barely Playable, Not Funny, Rampantly Offensive," *Ars Technica*, June 13, 2011. http://arstechnica.com.

8. Kuchera, "*Duke Nukem Forever*."

9. Jeffrey L. Wilson, "The 10 Most Violent Video Games of All Time," *PC Magazine*, June 3, 2012. www.pcmag.com.

10. Tom Orry, "*Killer7* Review," Videogamer, July 17, 2005. www.videogamer.com.

11. Doug Gross, "The 10 Biggest Violent Video-Game Controversies," "CNN Tech," CNN, June 29, 2011. http://articles.cnn.com.

12. Marc Saltzman, "*Grand Theft Auto: San Andreas*," CommonSense Media, 2012. www.commonsensemedia.org.

13. Quoted in Simon Carless, "ESRB Demands Publisher Audit for Hidden Game Content," GamaSutra, September 12, 2005. www.gamasutra.com.

14. Quoted in Gregg Toppo, "10 Years Later, the Real Story Behind Columbine," *USA Today*, April 14, 2009. www.usatoday.com.

15. Brian Ashcraft, "Creepy Jerk Arrested for Illicit Photos. He Tried to Blame Video Games," *Kotaku* (blog), May 24, 2012. http://kotaku.com.

Chapter Two: Do Violent Video Games Encourage Violent Acts?

16. Quoted in Steven Erlanger and Scott Shane, "Oslo Suspect Wrote of Fear of Islam and Plan for War," *New York Times*, July 23, 2011. www.nytimes.com.

17. Quoted in Helen Pidd, "Anders Breivik 'Trained for Shooting Attacks by Playing *Call of Duty*,'" *Guardian* (Manchester, UK), April 19, 2012. www.guardian.co.uk.

18. Quoted in Pidd, "Anders Breivik 'Trained for Shooting Attacks by Playing *Call of Duty*.'"

19. Quoted in Rhodri Marsden, "Is *World of Warcraft* Just Mindless Violence?," *Independent* (London), November 19, 2008. www.independent.co.uk.

20. Andrew Keen, "Does the Internet Breed Killers?," International Edition, CNN, April 19, 2012. http://edition.cnn.com.

21. Matt Peckham, "Norway Killer Played *World of Warcraft*, Which Probably Means Nothing at All," Techland, *Time*, April 17, 2012. http://techland.time.com.

22. Peckham, "Norway Killer Played *World of Warcraft*."

23. Tassi, "The Idiocy of Blaming Video Games for the Norway Massacre."

24. Christopher Ferguson, "Video Games Don't Make Kids Violent," Ideas, *Time*, December 7, 2011. http://ideas.time.com.

25. Ferguson, "Video Games Don't Make Kids Violent."

26. Ferguson, "Video Games Don't Make Kids Violent."

27. Quoted in Tom Law, "Anders Breivik: Did *Call of Duty* Really Influence the Norway Massacre?," *Sabotage Times*. www.sabotagetimes.com.

28. Tassi, "The Idiocy of Blaming Video Games for the Norway Massacre."

29. Quoted in Leung, "Can a Video Game Lead to Murder?"

30. Law, "Anders Breivik: Did *Call of Duty* Really Influence the Norway Massacre?"

31. Dave Grossman, "Teaching Kids to Kill," *National Forum*, Phi Kappa Phi, Fall 2000. www.killology.org.

32. Dave Grossman, "The Violent Video Game Plague," *Knowledge of Reality*, no. 17. www.sol.com.au.

33. Grossman, "Teaching Kids to Kill."

34. Quoted in Jeff Grabmeier, "Video Games Can Teach How to Shoot Guns More Accurately and Aim for the Head," Ohio State University Research Communications, April 30, 2012. http://re searchnews.osu.edu.

35. Quoted in Grabmeier, "Video Games Can Teach How to Shoot Guns More Accurately."

36. Quoted in Ted Gregory, "Big Game Hunting: A Former Soldier and Expert on Killing Sets His Sights on Violent Video Games," *Chicago Tribune*, July 25, 2000. http://articles.chicagotribune.com.

37. Henry Jenkins, "Reality Bytes: Eight Myths About Video Games Debunked," Impact of Gaming Essays, PBS. www.pbs.org.

38. Quoted in Leung, "Can a Video Game Lead to Murder?"

Chapter Three: Do Violent Video Games Promote Antisocial Behavior?

39. mf29, "Bully," Gamefaqs. www.gamefaqs.com.

40. Quoted in Ben Leapman and Jasper Copping, "Video Game Glorifies Bullying, Say Critics," *Telegraph* (London), January 20, 2008. www.telegraph.co.uk.

41. Quoted in Leapman and Copping, "Video Game Glorifies Bullying, Say Critics."

42. Quoted in Anthony Dixon, "'Bully' Video Game Met with Controversy," *Northern News*, 2008. www.northernnews.ca.

43. Kristin Kaining, "Will Controversy—or Quality—Sell 'Bully'?" MSNBC, November 2, 2006. www.msnbc.msn.com.

44. Quoted in Dixon, "'Bully' Video Game Met with Controversy."

45. Jenkins, "Reality Bytes: Eight Myths About Video Games Debunked."

46. Quoted in Michael Abbott, "In Praise of Empathy and Good Teaching," blog, Brainy Gamer, October 19, 2007. www.brainy gamer.com.

47. Abbott, "In Praise of Empathy and Good Teaching."

48. Quoted in Rick Nauert, "Video Games Desensitize to Real Violence," PsychCentral, July 28, 2006. http://psychcentral.com.

49. Quoted in Nauert, "Video Games Desensitize to Real Violence."

50. Quoted in TAMIU, "Violent Video Games Help Relieve Stress, Depression, Says TAMIU Professor," press release, June 17, 2010. www.tamiu.edu.

51. James Paul Gee, "Video Games: What They Can Teach Us About Audience Engagement," *Nieman Reports*, Summer 2010. www.nieman.harvard.edu.

52. Frank Mainwaring, "How Video Games Affect Our Lives," Helium, March 8, 2007. www.helium.com.

53. Mainwaring, "How Video Games Affect Our Lives."

54. mf29, "Bully."

55. Constance Steinkuehler, interview by Michel Martin, "What Can We Learn from Video Games?," transcript, NPR, April 18, 2012. www.npr.org.

56. Mainwaring, "How Video Games Affect Our Lives."

57. Mainwaring, "How Video Games Affect Our Lives."

58. Joey J. Lee and Christopher M. Hoadley, "'Ugly in a World Where You Can Choose to Be Beautiful': Teaching and Learning About Diversity via Virtual Worlds," paper presented at the International Conference of the Learning Sciences, 2006. www.tophe.net.

59. Brooke Bliven and Marin Abernethy, "Is Gaming Social Isolation?," blog, FYSM-126: Game Changers, October 19, 2010. http://fysm-126.wp.trincoll.edu.

Chapter Four: Do Violent Video Games Encourage Addictive Behavior?

60. Kirsten West Savali, "Philly Teen Murders Mother After She Takes Away His PlayStation," Black Voices, *Huffington Post*, February 18, 2011. www.bvblackspin.com.

61. Savali, "Philly Teen Murders Mother."

62. Jason Krell, "Video Game Addiction a Misnomer, More a Matter of Choice," *Daily Wildcat*, October 21, 20011, www.wildcat.arizona.edu.

63. Krell, "Video Game Addiction a Misnomer."

64. Grossman, "The Violent Video Game Plague."

65. Quoted in Leung, "Can a Video Game Lead to Murder?"

66. Rhodri Marsden, "Is *World of Warcraft* Just Mindless Violence?," *Independent* (London), July 20, 2012. www.independent.co.uk.

67. Quoted in Marsden, "Is *World of Warcraft* Just Mindless Violence?"

68. Nina Simon, "When Does Addictive Play Stop Being Valuable?," *Museum 2.0* (blog). http://museumtwo.blogspot.com.

69. Quoted in Luke Plunkett, "Former NFL Player Recovers from Video Game Addiction, Returns to Pro Football," *Kotaku* (blog), June 12, 2012. http://kotaku.com.

70. Quoted in Plunkett, "Former NFL Player Recovers from Video Game Addiction."

71. Ryan G. Van Cleave, "Why Johnny Can't Stop Playing Video Games," *Psychology Today*, November 8, 2010. www.psychology today.com.

72. Erin Hoffman, "Life, Addictive Game Mechanics, and the Truth Hiding in *Bejeweled*," GamaSutra.com, September 16, 2009. www.gamasutra.com.

73. David Wong, "5 Creepy Ways Video Games Are Trying to Get You Addicted," Cracked.com, March 8, 2010. www.cracked.com.

74. Wong, "5 Creepy Ways Video Games Are Trying to Get You Addicted."

75. Hoffman, "Life, Addictive Game Mechanics, and the Truth Hiding in *Bejeweled*."

76. Marsden, "Is *World of Warcraft* Just Mindless Violence?"

77. Quoted in Marsden, "Is *World of Warcraft* Just Mindless Violence?"

Chapter Five: Should the Sale of Violent Video Games Be Restricted?

78. Quoted in Dean Takahashi, "Governor Signs Bill on Violent Video Games," *San Jose Mercury News*, October 8, 2005.

79. Quoted in FoxNews.com, "Supreme Court Strikes Rule Banning Violent Video Game Sale to Kids," June 27, 2011. www.foxnews.com.

80. Quoted in NPR, "Court: California Can't Ban Violent Video Game Sales," June 27, 2011. www.npr.org

81. Quoted in FoxNews.com, "Supreme Court Strikes Rule Banning Violent Video Game Sale to Kids."

82. Quoted in Adam Liptak, "Justices Debate Video Game Ban," *New York Times*, November 2, 2010. www.nytimes.com.

83. Quoted in Joan Biskuic and Mike Snider, "Supreme Court Rejects Ban on Violent Video Games," *USA Today*, June 28, 2011. www.usatoday.com.

84. Quoted in Evan Narcisse, "Supreme Court: 'Video Games Qualify for First Amendment Protection,'" Techland, *Time*, June 27, 2011. http://techland.time.com.

85. Quoted in Narcisse, "Supreme Court: 'Video Games Qualify for First Amendment Protection.'"

86. Quoted in NPR, "Court: California Can't Ban Violent Video Game Sales."

87. Quoted in NPR, "Court: California Can't Ban Violent Video Game Sales."

88. Quoted in Alfred Hermida, "Parents 'Ignore Game Age Ratings,'" BBC News, June 24, 2005. http://news.bbc.co.uk.

89. Grossman, "The Violent Video Game Plague."

90. Leigh Alexander, "And You Thought *Grand Theft Auto* Was Bad: Should the United States Ban a Japanese 'Rape Simulator' Game?," *Slate*, March 9, 2009. www.slate.com.

91. Quoted in Leung, "Can a Video Game Lead to Murder?"

92. Kenneth Turan, "'Dark Knight Rises' Shooting: Skip the Blame Game and Take Action," *Los Angeles Times*, July 20, 2012. www.latimes.com.

93. Quoted in Steven Kent, *The Ultimate History of Video Games*. New York: Three Rivers, 2001, p. 92.

94. Quoted in Don Steinberg, "Adult Games Scoring Big with Children," *Philadelphia Inquirer*, December 1, 2002, p. A-1.

95. Evan Narcisse, "Games Rated 'Mature' Are Made Less, Bought More,'" Techland, *Time*, March 21, 2011. http://techland.time.com.

96. Turan, "'Dark Knight Rises' Shooting."

Related Organizations and Websites

Beatbullying
Rochester House
Units 1, 4 & 5
4 Belvedere Road
London SE19 2AT
email: info@beatbullying.org • website: www.beatbullying.org

This group supports anti-bullying efforts in the UK but also seeks to raise awareness worldwide regarding the need to do more to protect children from sex and violence in video games and on the Internet.

The Center for Successful Parenting Video Research Center
PO Box 3794
Carmel, Indiana 46082
email: csp@onrampamerica.net • website: www.sosparents.org

This group believes that video game violence can have a serious negative impact on children and seeks to educate parents about the dangers of gaming. It has also funded brain-scan research to study the physical effects of playing violent games.

Entertainment Software Association (ESA)

575 Seventh St. NW, Suite 300
Washington, DC 20004
e-mail: esa@theesa.com
website: www.theesa.com

A trade association, the ESA represents companies that publish and market video games and has been involved in legal efforts to fight the censorship of games and the restriction of their sales to minors.

Entertainment Software Rating Board (ESRB)

317 Madison Ave., 22nd Floor
New York, NY 10017
phone: (212) 759-0700
e-mail: info@esrb.org
website: www.esrb.org

Established by the Entertainment Software Association, the board oversees the voluntary ratings system whereby parents can determine which video games are appropriate for their children. The association's website also provides information about these ratings and the criteria the board uses to determine them.

Federal Trade Commission (FTC)

600 Pennsylvania Ave. NW
Washington, DC 20580
phone: (202) 326-2222
website: www.ftc.gov

The FTC is charged with protecting consumers, and to this end it has researched issues related to the purchase and playing of video games. Its website includes articles on video game ratings and video game violence.

Free Expression Policy Project (FEPP)

170 W. Seventy-Sixth St., #301
New York, NY 10023
website: www.fepproject.org

The FEPP is a think tank dedicated to opposing censorship and supporting those engaged in fighting for their First Amendment rights. Its website includes not only articles related to free speech but legal briefs and other documents related to First Amendment cases.

International Game Developers Association (IGDA)

19 Mantua Rd.
Mt. Royal, NJ 08061
phone: (856) 423-2990
fax: (856) 423-3420
e-mail: contact@igda.org
website: www.igda.org

The IGDA is a trade association supporting professionals who design and produce video games. It also advocates on issues affecting game designers.

Additional Reading

Books

Tom Bissell, *Extra Lives: Why Video Games Matter*. New York: Vintage, 2011.

Tristan Donovan, *Replay: The History of Video Games*. East Sussex, UK: Yellow Ant, 2010.

James Paul Gee and Elizabeth R. Hayes, *Women and Gaming: The Sims and 21st Century Learning*. New York: St. Martin's, 2010.

David M. Haugen and Susan Musser, eds., *Media Violence: Opposing Viewpoints*. Farmington Hills, MI: Greenhaven, 2009.

Steven J. Kirsh, *Media and Youth: A Developmental Perspective*. Oxford, UK: Wiley-Blackwell, 2009.

Bill Loguidice and Matt Barton, *Vintage Games: An Insider Look at the History of 'Grand Theft Auto,' 'Super Mario,' and the Most Influential Games of All Time*. Burlington, MA: Focal, 2009.

Jane McGonigal, *Reality Is Broken: Why Games Make Us Better and How They Can Change the World*. New York: Penguin, 2011.

Scott Rogers, *Level Up! The Guide to Great Video Game Design*. West Sussex, UK: John Wiley and Sons, 2010.

Ursula Smartt, *Media & Entertainment Law*. New York: Routledge, 2011.

Websites

Ars Technica (arstechnica.com). The *Ars Technica* online magazine provides articles about video gaming, technology, and Internet issues.

GamaSutra (www.gamasutra.com). This website provides information and articles about the art and business of making games.

GamePolitics (www.gamepolitics.com). Subtitled "Where Politics and Games Collide," Game Politics provides information about political issues related to video gaming.

The Gamer Widow (http://gamerwidow.com). This website offers support and information for the family members of people addicted to video games.

GameSpot (www.gamespot.com). This online game review site offers information on current video games.

Tech Addiction (www.techaddiction.ca). This Canadian site offers information and support for people suffering from video game and computer addictions.

Time Techland (http://techland.time.com). A part of the *Time* magazine website, this site provides news and reviews about video games.

Index

Note: Boldface page numbers indicate illustrations.

Picture Credits

About the Author

Patricia D. Netzley is the author of over fifty books for teens and adults. She also teaches writing and is a member of the Society of Children's Books Writers and Illustrators and the Romance Writers of America.